Constitutional Law

Second Edition

Cavendish
Publishing
Limited

London • Sydney

Second edition first published 1999 by Cavendish Publishing Limited, The Glass House, Wharton Street, London WC1X 9PX, United Kingdom

Telephone: + 44 (0)20 7278 8000

Facsimile: + 44 (0)20 7278 8080

Email: info@cavendishpublishing.com

Website: www.cavendishpublishing.com

British Library Cataloguing in Publication Data

Constitutional law – 2nd ed – (Law cards)

1 Constitutional law – Great Britain

342.4'1

ISBN 1 85941 500 8

Printed and bound in Great Britain

Contents

1 The citizen and the constitution

The constitutional jigsaw

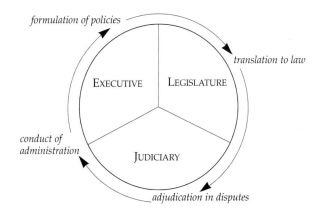

The numerous pieces within this jigsaw are the institutions of various shapes and sizes, which fit together via the constitution to provide a complete picture of government within our State. To facilitate the process of bringing these various institutional pieces together, we identify three areas into which these organs of State are located. These areas relate to the three branches of government: executive; legislature; and judiciary. The function of organs within the executive branch is to formulate policies and have conduct of administration within the state. The function of organs within the legislature is to legislate and thereby translate such policies into law. The task of the judicial branch is to adjudicate in instances of dispute and thereby enforce the laws of the State.

Sources of our constitutional law

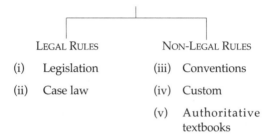

	LEGAL RULES		NON-LEGAL RULES
(i)	Legislation	(iii)	Conventions
(ii)	Case law	(iv)	Custom
		(v)	Authoritative textbooks

Constitutional law is the body of law which regulates the bringing together of these organs of state and identifies how they relate to each other. Its sources are both legal and non-legal, in the sense that some are capable of enforcement in a court of law whilst others, although legally recognised as being in existence, are not. The principal legal source of our constitutional law is legislation, both primary and secondary. In addition, our common law system places emphasis on judicial interpretations of the law in cases before the courts. The non-legal sources of our constitutional law includes constitutional conventions; customary rules relating both to the operation of Parliament and the Royal Prerogative and the writings of learned constitutional lawyers, whose authoritative interpretations on the operation of our constitution have in themselves become a part of it.

Types of constitution

WRITTEN   UNWRITTEN

A written constitution is one contained in one or a small group of documents. To many commentators, this offers the advantages of clarity, stability and enforceability over states with unwritten constitutions (that is, constitutions not to be found in one or a small group of documents).

Moreover, written constitutions are more readily accepted as enjoying the advantage of a prescriptive approach. In his article entitled 'The sound of silence: constitutional law without a constitution' (1994) LQR, Sir Stephen Sedley noted:

> ... in this country, we have constitutional law without having a constitution, not because our constitution is unwritten but because our constitutional law, historically at least, is merely descriptive: it offers an account of how the country has come to be governed.

However, there is little to suggest that a written constitution provides a better solution. Sir Stephen would acknowledge that a written constitution might even aggravate the problem for legislative and administrative experience would show 'that the more detail you try to prescribe, the less you find you have actually catered for'. No constitution can survive in the long term without recourse to the inherent descriptive flexibility of convention and practice.

Characteristics of our constitution

Rule of Law

RULE OF LAW SEPARATION OF POWERS INDEPENDENCE OF THE JUDICIARY PARLIAMENTARY SOVEREIGNTY

One of the central characteristics of our constitution, according to Professor AV Dicey, is our adherence to the concept of the Rule of Law. In 'The Rule of Law in Britain today' (1989), the Constitutional Reform Centre noted that Dicey held it to be essential to the Rule of Law that public authorities should be subject to the same law as the ordinary citizen, administered in the ordinary courts, and many of the European systems of law (based on the Roman law tradition) failed the test in giving the State a special position in law. But, such a stringent definition is too narrow in that, even within our common law system, the State may be seen to occupy a special position.

The importance of this concept to the workings of our constitution is given further consideration in Chapter 3 when we explore the constitutional significance of *M v Home Office ex p Baker* (1993).

Separation of powers/independence of the judiciary
The concept of the Rule of Law is not alone in attempting to check the potential for arbitrary government. The concept of the separation of powers also seeks to attain this purpose by

segregating both the functions and personnel of the three branches of government: executive; legislature; and judiciary. In the UK, we seek to achieve the independence of our judiciary by offering senior judges security of tenure under the Act of Settlement 1700, so that they might dispense justice without fear or favour. But, our judiciary is not wholly independent of the executive and legislature and, as the Constitutional Reform Centre pointed out, we have a weak judicial branch, 'perhaps the weakest in any country where the Rule of Law can be said to operate'.

The significance of these concepts to the working of our constitution was recently illustrated in the decision of *Re Pinochet Ugarte* (1999). On an earlier decision, the House of Lords had decided by a majority of three to two that the State Immunity Act 1978 did not protect General Pinochet of Chile from extradition to Spain to face criminal charges. However, in an unprecedented move this decision had to be set aside by the House of Lords as Lord Hoffman (one of the majority judges), by virtue of his relationship with Amnesty International, was effectively acting as a judge in his own cause. A new panel of seven judges was required to hear the case afresh. This case caused some commentators to question whether our judiciary is moving away from purely impartial precedent based decision making to more 'political' deliberation.

Parliamentary sovereignty
This is because our constitution is based upon the common law rule of parliamentary sovereignty. This means that Parliament is not only competent to legislate upon any subject matter and cannot be bound by its predecessors but also once Parliament has legislated no court can pass judgment upon the validity of that legislation. Thus, unlike

the constitution of the USA with its adherence to the separation of powers, we do not have a Supreme Court with the capacity to declare legislation 'unconstitutional' and therefore devoid of legal effect. Moreover, the constitutional position of our judicial branch is further weakened by the near complete fusion of our executive and legislative branches. Parliament has historically been concerned with checking the power of the executive by making it accountable for its actions. However, this accountability has been eroded leading to the executive coming to dominate Parliament to such an extent that in 1978 the House of Commons Select Committee on Procedure concluded that:

> ... the balance of advantage between Parliament and government in the day to day working of the constitution is now weighted in favour of the government to a degree which arouses widespread anxiety and is inimical to the proper working of our parliamentary democracy.

European Union

Road to Union

In 1948, the Organisation for Economic Co-operation and Development (OECD) was established with financial assistance from the USA in order to regenerate the economies of Europe after the Second World War. This was followed in 1949 with the creation of the North Atlantic Treaty Organisation or NATO (a military alliance between Europe and the USA and Canada) and the Council of Europe, from which we now have the European Convention on Human Rights (ECHR).

Initiated by Robert Schuman, the French Foreign Minister, 1951 saw the creation of the European Coal and Steel Community (ECSC) under the Treaty of Paris, and the European Atomic Energy Community (EURATOM) under the Treaty of Rome in 1957, providing for a supra-national regulation of the non-military use of atomic energy.

An additional Treaty of Rome signed in 1957 saw the creation of the European Economic Community (Common Market) with an original membership of six States.

The concept of a unified common trading market, visualised in this Treaty of Rome 1957, was realised in the UK under the Single European Act 1986. In February 1992, the Maastricht Treaty on European Union was signed, coming into force in this country in November 1993. The Treaty organised the now European Union into three pillars. The *first* pillar amended the EEC Treaty, making it the EC Treaty. The *second* pillar provided for a series of statements of intent on a common foreign and security policy. The *third* provided for a common policy on justice and home affairs.

The Maastricht Treaty therefore created a European Union and was followed by the launch, on 1 January 1999, of a Single European Currency, the Euro.

Whereas decision making in pillars two and three is achieved through inter-governmental co-operation, the first pillar is regulated by community law via the institutions of the Community. These Community Institutions are the Council of Ministers, the European Commission, the Parliament and the European Court of Justice. However, all three pillars are headed by the European Council under which Heads of Government and Foreign Ministers meet twice a year to formulate major policy decisions.

In January 1999, the European Commission faced a censure motion in the European Parliament over allegations of corruption and fraud in the Union. This led to the setting up of a Committee of 'Wise Men' to investigate the matter. Following this Committee's report, all 20 commissioners collectively resigned in March 1999.

Subsidiarity

One of the most important legal developments introduced by the Maastricht Treaty on European Union was the concept of subsidiarity. Article 3b (now Art 5) of the Maastricht Treaty on European Union provides that:

> The community shall act within the limits of the powers conferred upon it by this Treaty and of the objectives assigned to it therein. In areas which do not fall within its exclusive competence, the community shall take action, in accordance with the principle of subsidiarity, only if and in so far as the objectives of the proposed action cannot be sufficiently achieved by the Member States and can therefore, by reason of the scale or effects of the proposed action, be better achieved by the community.

> Any action by the community shall not go beyond what is necessary to achieve the objectives of this Treaty.

The principle of the attribution of powers, contained in the first part of the Article, requires that the community is only entitled to act when it is given the express power to do so.

This principle is supplemented by the key concept of subsidiarity. According to this principle, as it may be understood in its strict legal sense, the community not only has to justify its ability to act, but also justify why it and not the Member State should act. There is, however, an important qualification on the operation of this principle in that it cannot be applied to matters falling within the community's exclusive competence, sometimes referred to as the *occupied field*. In short, it is only intended to operate in relation to those areas where the community has a parallel competence with Member States.

The third principle, that of proportionality or intensity found in the last paragraph of the Article, applies not only to areas of parallel competence, but also to areas of exclusive competence. It requires that the intensity of community action must always be in proportion to the objective being pursued.

Treaty of Amsterdam 1997

Proposals are under consideration for the expansion of the European Union from its present membership of 15 States to 27. Primarily in response to this prospect of further expansion, the Member States of the European Union met in Amsterdam on 16 and 17 June 1997 to draw up a new Treaty for European Union, building upon the opportunities created by the Maastricht Treaty 1992. This Treaty came into force in the UK in May 1999 and, in addition to renumbering Articles, has the effect of amending the workings of the European Union. One of the main reforms of this Treaty is to simplify the decision making procedures within the European Union. To this end, the elected European Parliament will have increased decision making powers, the appointment of the Commission President is made subject to the European Parliament's formal approval, the number of European Commissioners will be reduced to a maximum of one

Commissioner per Member State, areas where decisions can be taken by a qualified majority are extended and closer ties with national Parliaments are encouraged.

In addition to preparing for further expansion, the latest Treaty also contains provisions which provide for placing employment and citizens' rights at the heart of the European Union. It also aims to provide for a stronger voice for the European Union in future world affairs.

Factortame *litigation*

The significance of our membership of the European Union to our constitutional law may be gauged by its impact on our concept of parliamentary sovereignty. On becoming a member of the European Community in 1973, the UK was subject to Art 189 (now Art 249) which holds regulations and directives to be binding upon all Member States. In addition, Art 5 (now Art 10) requires that Member States agree 'to ensure fulfilment of (their treaty) obligations'. An example of the supremacy of Community law can be seen in the *Factortame* litigation.

Factortame was a company of mostly Spanish directors and shareholders which owned and operated 95 vessels from the UK. Although previously registered under the Merchant Shipping Act 1894, the vessels were no longer capable of registration under the stringent Merchant Shipping (Registration of Fishing Vessels) Regulations made under the new Merchant Shipping Act 1988. In particular, the new regulations required the whole of the legal title and at least 75% of beneficial ownership to be vested in UK citizens (that is, domiciled in the UK) or UK companies (that is, principal place of business in the UK). The company applied for a judicial review to challenge the validity of the regulations and a preliminary ruling from the European Court of Justice was sought under Art 177. Pending the ruling and by way of interim relief, judges in the Divisional Court disapplied the new regulations. The Secretary of State appealed and judges in the Court of Appeal set aside the order for interim relief, a decision upheld by judges in the House of Lords. However, the judges in the House of Lords also sought a preliminary ruling on the granting of interim relief.

In the meantime, the Commission brought an action against the UK for a declaration that the nationality provisions contained within the new regulations were in breach of the then Arts 52 and 221 of the Treaty of Rome. The European Court of Justice held that the aim of the common fisheries policy did not warrant the new regulations, which the UK were obliged to amend by Order in Council in 1989. On the issue of the request for a preliminary ruling from the House of Lords, the European Court of Justice ruled that a court which would have granted interim relief but for a rule of domestic law should set aside that rule of domestic law in favour of observing treaty obligations. Thus, on matters involving a European element, a duly passed Act of Parliament may now be effectively set aside by a UK court if it considers that the statute may violate Community law.

Such decisions have led judges, such as Hoffman J in *Stoke-on-Trent CC v B & Q* (1991), to conclude that our treaty obligations to the European Union are 'the supreme law of this country, taking precedence over Acts of Parliament'.

'Programme' of constitutional reform

From the position of a constitutional law student, the General Election of 1 May 1997 is of considerable significance, in as much as it produced a government which has pledged major constitutional reform.

At the Annual Constitutional Unit Lecture delivered in December 1998, the Lord Chancellor, Lord Irvine of Lairg, described the New Labour government's prescription for constitutional change as 'a major programme of constitutional change realigning the most fundamental relationships between the State and the individual ... our objective is to put in place an integrated programme of measures to decentralise power on the UK; and to enhance the rights of individuals within a more open society'.

Claiming the government's incremental approach to be one of 'pragmatism based on principle', Lord Irvine identified the reform programme as being:

- the new Human Rights Act 1998;

- devolution for Scotland, Wales and Northern Ireland;

- elected regional government for England, subject to popular demand;

- an elected Mayor and separate Assembly for London;

- uniform structure for local government;

- modernisation of the House of Commons;

- reform of the House of Lords;

- a new Freedom of Information Act;

- new electoral systems.

The significance of these changes is illustrated when we consider their impact in the following chapters.

2 The citizen and the legislature

The Queen in Parliament

(Upper) HOUSE OF LORDS   (Lower) HOUSE OF COMMONS

In this chapter, we will study the role performed by Parliament and in so doing recognise that the *Queen in Parliament* is the supreme law making power within our state. Parliament is bicameral, in that it consists of two legislative chambers. The House of Lords is still referred to as the *Upper* House. At one time, this accurately reflected its significance in relation to the other chamber, the House of Commons. But, the continuing growth in democracy within our State led to the *lower chamber*, as the only elected chamber, acquiring increasing significance until, at the beginning of this century, it successfully challenged the Upper House for constitutional supremacy.

House of Lords

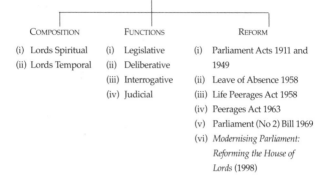

COMPOSITION	FUNCTIONS	REFORM
(i) Lords Spiritual	(i) Legislative	(i) Parliament Acts 1911 and 1949
(ii) Lords Temporal	(ii) Deliberative	(ii) Leave of Absence 1958
	(iii) Interrogative	(iii) Life Peerages Act 1958
	(iv) Judicial	(iv) Peerages Act 1963
		(v) Parliament (No 2) Bill 1969
		(vi) *Modernising Parliament: Reforming the House of Lords* (1998)

In States which claim to be representative democracies, the usual constitutional mechanism employed to ensure accountability to the public is that of elections. Yet, we have already noted that one of our parliamentary chambers, the House of Lords, is presently unelected. Thus, under our constitution, we have a government, predominantly from the elected chamber, which is made accountable for its actions to an unaccountable chamber. This ultimately led to the removal of the chambers legislative power of veto over primary legislation under the Parliament Act 1911. Under this Act, government Bills could be enacted without the consent of the House of Lords which now only had a power to delay legislation for three successive sessions (two years). This delaying power was reduced, under the Parliament Act 1949 to two successive sessions (one year). Moreover, Bills certified as 'Money Bills' by the Speaker could attain royal assent direct from the House of Commons, if they had been placed before the House of Lords for a minimum period of a month. But, this is not to say that the Upper House is not without power or significance today.

Some would argue that the power and influence of the House of Lords stems from the fact that members of the chamber do not have an electorate to please. This, combined with a less domineering party whip system, ensures a greater degree of independence. Thus, its members are perhaps more readily able to view things in terms of the national interest than their elected colleagues, who are obliged to take constituency and party interests into account. The composition of the House of Lords may, therefore, be seen both as its weakness and its strength. But, will the House of Lords remain wholly unelected?

Reform of the House of Lords

The composition of the House of Lords on 2 November 1998 was as follows:

Archbishops and bishops	26	
Peers by succession	750	(16 women)
Hereditary peers of first creation	9	
Life peers under the Appellate Jurisdiction Act 1876	28	
Life peers under the Life Peerages Act 1958	485	(87 women)
	1,298	

Moreover, declared party allegiances within the House at the same date were:

Party	Life Peers	Hereditary Peers		Lords Spiritual	Total
		Of First Creation	By Succession		
Conservative	173	4	298		475
Labour	158	1	17		176
Liberal Dem	45	0	24		69
Cross Bench	120	4	198		322
Other	9	0	87	26	122
Total	**505**	**9**	**624**	**26**	**1,164**

The present government has pledged to remove the right to sit and vote of hereditary peers. The Prime Minister, Tony Blair, affirmed 'for too long, hereditary peers with no democratic legitimacy, whose role is based on birth and not merit, have been able to play a part in passing laws affecting everyone in Britain'.

Pragmatism and comprise have resulted in the government phasing in this reform. Nevertheless, the government is intent on achieving this change in composition as a first step towards a radical overhaul of the Upper House. Options for a radical overhaul of the second chamber, affecting both its composition and constitutional role, are contained in the government's White Paper, *Modernising Parliament: Reforming the House of Lords* (1998). These options are to be explored in detail by a Royal Commission on the Reform of the House of Lords, which has been set up under the chairmanship of Lord Wakeham and is required to report its findings by the end of 1999. After consideration by a Joint Committee of both Houses of Parliament, the government will respond to the recommendations of the Royal Commission before the next general election.

House of Commons

COMPOSITION

(i) Electoral law and systems

FUNCTIONS

(i) Accountability via debate

(ii) Accountability via questioning and investigation

(iii) Accountability via scrutiny of national finance

Does the fact that the House of Commons is elected mean it is democratic, in the sense that its members may be said to truly represent the wishes of the electorate?

Consider the General Election results from 1979 to 1997:

		1979	1983	1987	1992	1997
Labour	votes (%)	36.9	27.6	30.8	34.5	44.4
	seats (%)	42.2	32.2	35.2	41.6	63.6
Conservative	votes (%)	43.9	42.4	42.2	41.9	31.4
	seats (%)	53.4	61.1	57.8	51.6	25.0
Liberal(*)	votes (%)	13.8	25.4	22.6	17.9	17.2
	seats (%)	1.7	3.5	3.4	3.1	7.0
Others	votes (%)	5.5	4.6	4.4	5.7	7.0
	seats (%)	2.7	3.2	3.5	3.7	4.4

(*) 1979: Liberal; 1983 and 1987: Liberal/SDP; 1992 and 1997: Liberal Democrats

It may be seen from these results that no government managed to achieve over 50% of the votes cast, yet always achieved over 50% of the seats in the House of Commons. By contrast, the Liberal Democrat vote always exceeded 10% but never secured 10% of the seats. The reason for these anomalies arises from the way in which our *first-past-the-post* electoral system reflects strong centralised support within a constituency but fails to reflect support for parties diluted over a wide range of constituencies. The targeting of marginal constituencies in 1997 accounted for the Liberal Democrats doubling their number of seats from 1992 with a smaller percentage of the vote.

Electoral reform

Following its electoral success in May 1997, the new Labour government set up an Independent Commission in

December of the same year to consider alternatives to the first-past-the post system for general elections.

Under the chairmanship of Lord Jenkins, the Independent Commission was invited to observe four requirements: broad proportionality; the need for stable government; an extension of voter choice; and maintaining the link between an MP and a geographical constituency. The Independent Commission looked at four different systems of election and graded each in accordance with these criteria as follows:

	First Past the Post	Alternative Vote	Additional Member System	Single Transferable Vote System
Proportionality	1	2	5	4
Stable government	4	3	2	2
Voter choice	1	3	3	5
Constituency link	5	5	3	3

(1 lowest, 5 highest)

In its report published in 1998, the Independent Commission on the voting system recommended a two vote mixed system. 80–85% of MPs would still be elected to represent a single member geographical constituency, but under the alternative vote system of election not the present first-past-the-post system. The remaining 15–20% of MPs would be elected regionally on a top-up basis to mitigate any disproportionality in these constituency results.

A different electoral system to the first-past-the-post system was used for the inaugural Scottish Parliament and Welsh Assembly elections on 6 May 1999. In Scotland, 73 MSPs were elected from single member constituencies under first-past-the-post with an additional 56 'top-up' MSPs elected from regional party lists. Likewise, in Wales, 40 AMs were elected from single member constituencies under first-past-the-post, and an additional 20 AMs elected from regional party lists. The June 1999 European Parliament Elections will, for the first time, use a regional list form of Proportional Representation (based upon the d'Hondt formula).

Differing electoral systems are also envisaged for the Northern Ireland Assembly (using the single transferable vote system to vote in six members for each of the 18 constituencies), the Greater London Authority Assembly, and the election for the office of Mayor of London.

The government itself remains undisturbed by the number of different electoral systems either already in play or about to come into play. Their argument is that no election system is perfect and each has to be assessed in relation to the elected institution concerned.

However, the most important election in our system of government remains as that to the Westminster Parliament and a referendum on the Jenkins' proposals is awaited.

Accountability via debate

The concept of parliamentary sovereignty demands that Parliament has no legislative rival. The supremacy of Parliament in making law needs to be considered, however, within the context of the convention of ministerial responsibility (considered in more detail in Chapter 3).

This important convention of our constitution recognises that, far from separating the personnel within our executive from the legislature, our constitution requires, with the notable exception of the civil service, that members of our executive are drawn exclusively from the legislature. This overlap between the two branches is regarded by some as essential to the efficient operation of our constitution. This is because the convention demands that the legislative programme of the government of the day must command the confidence of the legislature, without which the government is collectively obliged to resign. It is logical, therefore, for convention to also require that the Monarch appoint as Prime Minister a person able to command a majority in Parliament.

On the face of it, this would seem to demonstrate considerable power on the part of our Parliament within the constitution. The very survival of the government turns on its day to day support for their legislative programme. But, this very fact has led to developments within our constitution which counter-balance the inherent instability this poses.

We should recognise that much has happened within the House of Commons to ensure that the government of the day can count upon its legislative support. With the growth in enfranchisement and universal adult suffrage came the corresponding growth in political parties. Originating as a loose association of like-minded individuals elected to office, these political parties soon developed an infrastructure and *whip system*. The purpose of the whip system was and still is to maximise party effect by ensuring a disciplined collective vote on legislative matters.

One might consider that it is not unreasonable for a government comprised of ministers drawn exclusively from members of one political party, predominantly within the House of Commons, to expect the support of colleagues committed to implementing the same election manifesto. Nevertheless, there has been criticism that the demands of party loyalty have done much to undermine the *individuality* of our elected representatives, who far from calling the executive to account for their legislative proposals may be seen to act as mere lobby fodder for the party machine they serve.

It may be argued that MPs do have a role to play in initiating debate within Parliament on matters of national or constituency interest. Standing Orders provide an opportunity to initiate an emergency debate, propose a Bill under the Ten Minute Rule and sponsor a Private Members' Bill. Furthermore, at the end of a day's business, members may initiate an adjournment debate on local or personal issues. Parliamentary time is, however, at a premium, and it is the task of the Leader of the House to ensure that such time as is available is maximised to ensure the smooth passage of the governments legislative programme for the parliamentary session. To this end, the government has considerable procedural powers at its disposal including the *guillotine*, under which the time made available for debate at one or more stages of a bill can be restricted.

The various legislative stages undertaken by government bills on matters of public importance include: first reading (formal introduction of the proposal); second reading (where the principles of the bill are considered and a vote taken at committee stage (where a standing committee scrutinises the Bill in detail); report stage (where the chair of the standing committee reports to the House on the committees deliberations); and the third reading and vote which completes the Bill's passage through the House of Commons and denotes its progression to 'the other place'. Although procedures do vary, the stages in the House of

Lords are much the same. Once the Bill has received a third reading in the House of Lords, it is presented for royal assent which, by convention, should not be withheld.

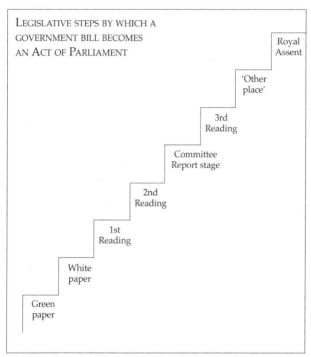

LEGISLATIVE STEPS BY WHICH A
GOVERNMENT BILL BECOMES
AN ACT OF PARLIAMENT

Royal Assent

'Other place'

3rd Reading

Committee Report stage

2nd Reading

1st Reading

White paper

Green paper

Different parliamentary stages, however, apply to Private Bills (which are promoted by individuals or bodies to give powers in addition to or varying from the general law) and Hybrid Bills (in essence, a Public Bill specifically affecting an individuals private rights).

Whereas the principle of the legislation is often contained within a statute, much of the fine detail of its law will be enacted through delegated legislation. There are different types of delegated legislation to which different levels of parliamentary scrutiny apply. Two interesting developments in this regard have been Standing Order 101, which provides for one or more standing committees in the House of Commons for the consideration of delegated legislation, and the recent creation of a Select Committee on the Scrutiny of Delegated Power for the House of Lords. When recommending the creation of this Committee, the Procedure Committee noted: '... democracy is not only about the election of politicians, but about setting limits to their powers.'

The most common types of delegated or subordinate legislation are Statutory Instruments (see Statutory Instruments Act 1946) and Orders in Council. It is important to note that many of the directives eminating from the European Union are implemented into our law via delegated legislation.

Accountability via questioning and investigation

One of the more visible demonstrations of a minister's accountability to Parliament is the practice of requiring the minister to come on a regular basis to answer oral questions from backbench MPs on the operation of their department. This demonstration of our parliamentary democracy in action, which in the case of the Prime Minister has recently been limited to once a week, may provide an interesting spectacle for the recent broadcasting of proceedings but the practice is of limited value in calling the executive to account for its action. In addition to oral questions, backbench MPs may also, and more usually pose, written questions to ministers often relating to a constituent's grievance.

In recognition of the limited effectiveness of parliamentary scrutiny by questioning, the all party Select Committee on Procedure recommended in 1978 that a new system of departmental select committees be introduced to scrutinise the 'policy, administration and finance' of a shadowed department of state. When introducing this reform shortly after the general election in 1979, the Leader of the House, Norman St John-Stevas (now Lord St John-Stevas), announced to the House of Commons that, 'after years of discussion and debate, we are embarking upon a series of changes that could constitute the most important parliamentary reforms of the century'.

There were, therefore, high hopes in 1979 that this new system of investigative committees would do much to redress the balance of power between Parliament and the executive, to enable the House of Commons to do more effectively the job it has been elected to do. But, to what extent has this potential been realised today?

A case study in the present day limitations of a departmental select committee investigation is provided by contrasting the investigation of the relevant select committee with the Scott Inquiry into the 'Arms to Iraq affair'. The 1800 page Scott Report, published in February 1996, made a number of important findings, not least of which were that Parliament had been 'deliberately' misled by government ministers, the Matrix Churchill trial 'ought never to have commenced'; nevertheless, the government had no intention of sending innocent men to jail by blocking the release of crucial documents during the trial.

In his assessment of the Scott Report, Professor Vernon Bogdanor noted: '... perhaps the deepest lesson of the Scott Inquiry is that Parliament is in danger of losing its capacity to bring ministers to account.' In response to sentiments of this nature, new rules were applied in January 1997 for persons giving evidence before its committees, in an attempt by Parliament to strengthen its position.

Accountability via scrutiny of national finance

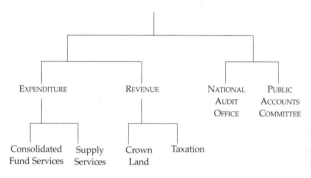

Our system of national finance may be viewed as amounting to little more than '*the Crown demands money, the Commons grants it and the Lords assents to the grant*'. Others might argue, however, that, in running our nation's finances, the executive remains effectively accountable to Parliament in two important respects. In the first instance, only Parliament has the legal authority to sanction public expenditure and revenue. Secondly, it is the ultimate responsibility of Parliament to ensure that any expenditure which has been sanctioned is both properly and efficiently spent.

In terms of spending, public expenditure takes the two forms of consolidated fund services and supply services. Consolidated fund services relate to charges on the *public revenue* or *public funds* under 'Permanent Acts' which give a continuing authority to pay for these services out of the Consolidated Fund or National Loans Fund. Supply services relate to charges paid out of *money provided by Parliament* which requires a specific statutory authority to pay for the service out of the Consolidated Fund or National Loans Fund.

In terms of raising money to pay for national expenditure, some revenue is derived from Crown land (which is given to the state in return for the civil list) but the vast majority is raised through the imposition of taxes. Some taxation is authorised by Parliament in the form of 'Permanent Acts', which remain in force until repealed or amended. Stamp duty and vat would be examples of this. Other taxes, such as income tax and customs and excise duties, are, however, authorised by 'Annual Acts' which remain in force for a year and, as *charges upon the people*, are part of *ways and means business*.

In 1993, the parliamentary expenditure (supply services) cycle and the parliamentary revenue (ways and means) cycle were reformed. The new procedure dovetails projected expenditure and proposed revenue into one joint proposal, which is passed by Parliament prior to the commencement of the new financial year in April.

Whereas it must be said that parliamentary support for the government's proposals on expenditure and taxation will divide along party lines, the same cannot be said of parliamentary scrutiny of how the executive spends public money. The National Audit Act 1983 had as its purpose the strengthening of parliamentary supervision over expenditure by providing for a National Audit Office, headed by a Comptroller and Auditor General, and the establishment of a Public Accounts Commission. The intention is that these bodies should work with the Public Accounts Committee of the House of Commons to promote economy, efficiency and effectiveness in the use of public money.

In January 1994, the all party Public Accounts Committee produced an unprecedented report criticising the growth in waste and corruption within the public sector. The committees stated in its report:

> ... in recent years, we have seen and reported on a number of serious failures in administrative and financial systems and controls within departments and other public bodies, which have led to money being wasted or otherwise improperly spent ... these failings represent a departure from the standards of public conduct which have mainly been established during the last 140 years (the Northcote-Trevelyan Report having exposed nepotism and incompetence in our civil service 140 years ago).

Parliamentary privilege

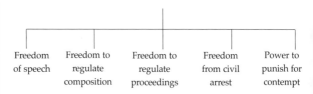

| Freedom of speech | Freedom to regulate composition | Freedom to regulate proceedings | Freedom from civil arrest | Power to punish for contempt |

Parliamentary privilege is part of the law and custom of Parliament. We are informed by Erskine May that it is a necessary requirement of our constitution for, without it, MPs 'could not discharge their functions'. The most important privilege, freedom of speech and debate, is claimed under Art 9 of the Bill of Rights 1689 which provides that 'freedom of speech and debates or proceedings in Parliament ought not to be impeached or questioned in any court or place out of Parliament'. The issue of what is covered by the term *proceedings in Parliament* was raised in the case of *GR Strauss* (1958).

Other privileges enjoyed by MPs include their collective right to regulate both the chamber's composition and proceedings. Whereas the determination of election petitions have now been transferred to an election court presided over by judges, the case of *Gary Allighan* (1947) clearly demonstrates a power to expel a duly elected member from the chamber. Following the General Election of 1 May 1997, both Gerry Adams and Martin McGuinness of Sinn Fein were banned by the Speaker from taking up their seats in the House of Commons. This was as a direct result of their refusal to take the Oath of Allegiance to the Crown. In addition, the cases of *Bradlaugh v Gossett* (1884) and *R v Graham-Campbell ex p Herbert* (1935) can also be used to demonstrate judicial acceptance of the notion that members have a right to claim exclusive cognisance over all internal matters.

Whereas emphasis is not unnaturally given to the privileges enjoyed by MPs, it should not be forgotten that parliamentary privilege also extends to the other chamber in the legislature. For example, despite its recommended abolition by the Committee on Parliamentary Privilege in

1967, members of the House of Lords, like their legislative colleagues in the House of Commons, still enjoy freedom from civil arrest.

In the past, Parliament has always claimed to be the sole and absolute judge of its own privileges. Evidence for this can be seen in the case of *Stockdale v Hansard* (1839) and the related *Case of the Sheriff of Middlesex* (1840). Difficulties arose here because the courts maintained a right to determine the nature and limit of parliamentary privilege where it affected the rights of individuals outside Parliament. Whereas this matter had eventually to be settled by the passing of the Parliamentary Papers Act 1840, an interesting development in this area can be seen in the case of *Rost v Edwards* (1990). In this case, Popplewell J stated that where there is uncertainty as to whether Parliament or the courts have jurisdiction over an issue of parliamentary privilege the courts should 'not be astute to find a reason for ousting the jurisdiction of the court and for limiting or even defeating a proper claim by a party to litigation before it'.

The case of *Allason v Haines* (1995) illustrates further difficulties which have arisen in the courts resultant from claims to parliamentary privilege. In following the decision of the Privy Council in *Prebble v Television New Zealand* (1994), Owen J was content to stay a libel action brought by an MP on the grounds that parliamentary privilege prevented the defendants putting forward their defence.

Despite warnings from Lord Simon that 'it is nearly impossible to exaggerate the constitutional importance of changes to parliamentary privilege', changes were in consequence made to the effect of Art 9 of the Bill of Rights 1689 under s 13 of the Defamation Act 1996. Where the conduct of a person in, or in relation to proceedings in, Parliament is an issue in defamation proceedings, those Parliamentary proceedings can now be questioned in the court. However, there can be no liability for words spoken or things done in the course of any proceedings in Parliament and this exception to Art 9 of the Bill of Rights 1689 is limited to issues of defamation.

Standards of conduct

THE 'SEVEN PRINCIPLES' OF PUBLIC LIFE

Selflessness · Integrity · Objectivity · Accountability · Openness · Honesty · Leadership

Selflessness
Holders of public office should take decisions solely in terms of the public interest. They should not do so in order to gain financial or other benefits for themselves, their family or their friends.

Integrity
Holders of public office should not place themselves under any financial or other obligation to outside individuals or organisations that might influence them in the performance of their official duties.

Objectivity

In carrying out public business, including making public appointments, awarding contracts, or recommending individuals for rewards and benefits, holders of public office should make choices on merit.

Accountability

Holders of public office are accountable for their decisions and actions to the public and must submit themselves to whatever scrutiny is appropriate to their office.

Openness

Holders of public office should be as open as possible about all the decisions and actions that they take. They should give reasons for their decisions and restrict information only when the wider public interest clearly demands.

Honesty

Holders of public office have a duty to declare any private interests relating to their public duties and to take steps to resolve any conflicts arising in a way that protects the public interest.

Leadership

Holders of public office should promote and support these principles by leadership and example.

In its Report on the '*Sunday Times* cash for questions affair', the Committee of Privileges found that the conduct of members who tabled parliamentary questions in return for payment, 'fell short of the standards' expected by the House. Of the two members involved, one was formally reprimanded and suspended for 20 days without pay and the other reprimanded and suspended for 10 days. In response to this and a general concern about 'sleaze' in public life, the Committee on Standards in Public Life was established in October 1994 to act, in the words of the then Prime Minister, John Major, as 'an ethical workshop' providing 'running repairs on standards in public life'.

The Committee's first report under the chairmanship of Lord Nolan was published in May 1995, and made important recommendations for the reform of Parliament. In particular, it was proposed that the rules on disclosure of members' interests should be tightened up and regulated by a new Parliamentary Commissioner for Standards (first appointed in November 1995) and that members of the House of Commons be prohibited from entering into paid advocacy agreements on behalf of private companies.

In October 1997, Sir Patrick Neill was appointed to succeed Lord Nolan as Chairman. To date, the Committee on Standards in Public Life has produced five reports, with the last Report on the funding of political parties requiring an expansion in the terms of reference.

It remains to be seen whether this Committee can live up to Professor Peter Hennessy's billing as 'a miniature, if informal, constitutional convention'.

Parliamentary Commissioner for Administration

PUBLIC	PRIVATE
Parliamentary Commissioner for Administration (PCA)	Banks
	Building Societies
Health Service	Estate Agents
Local Government	Insurance
Courts and Legal Services	Investment
Prisons	Pensions
Parliamentary Commissioner for Standards	
European Commissioner	

In order to facilitate the work of backbench MPs, the government of the day in 1967 acceded to a proposal contained within the Whyatt Report 1962 to create the office of the Parliamentary Commissioner for Administration, perhaps better known as the Ombudsman (Scandinavian for '*grievance man*'). In introducing what was to become the Parliamentary Commissioner for Administration Act 1967, the relevant minister, Richard Crossman, welcomed the introduction of an official who was intended to provide 'a cutting edge' for MPs investigating maladministration within the executive branch of State.

The creation of this 'grievance man' heralded the start in the growth of an Ombudsman 'system'. In addition to giving the Parliamentary Commissioner the dual function of looking at administration within the Health Service, new

Ombudsfolk were created for local government (first in Northern Ireland then for England and Wales and finally Scotland). New Ombudsmen continue to be created. Under the Courts and Legal Services Act 1990, the office of Legal Services Ombudsman was created. Moreover, these statutory ombudsfolk have been joined by a growing band of colleagues supervising the private sector.

The creation of the office of the Parliamentary Commissioner for Administration may have been the catalyst for these subsequent developments but the question can be posed: to what extent has this original office fulfilled its intended purpose?

In their article, 'A "cutting edge"? The Parliamentary Commissioner and MPs' (1990) 53 MLR 758, Professor Gavin Drewry and Professor Carol Harlow concluded: 'Crossman's description of the Parliamentary Commissioner as the "cutting-edge" of the backbenchers' complaints service looks today like empty rhetoric'.

Of the representative sample of MPs interviewed by Drewry and Harlow, 67% described the office as being of only slight value to them and 11% believed it to be of no value to them whatsoever. The research revealed that, 'for too many MPs, the [Ombudsman] has no *raison d'être*', and, together with their staff, they relate more to the civil servants whose work they are called upon to investigate than MPs whose servants they ultimately are.

It may be thought that the services provided by the Ombudsman would have formed an important part in the government's *Citizen's Charter: Raising the Standard* (1991). The work of the Ombudsman in fact receives scant attention and emphasis was given instead to a system of 'lay adjudicators'. In an article, 'A new breed of ombudsperson?' (1993) PL, Professor Dawn Oliver noted that 'the Adjudicator, unlike the Parliamentary Commissioner for Administration, is not directly accountable to the House of Commons and has no direct link with the House'. Professor Oliver concluded that this represented 'an interesting departure from the traditional monopoly of "redress of grievance" functions by the Commons'.

More recently, the Select Committee on the Parliamentary Commissioner for Administration undertook a far reaching inquiry into the powers, work and jurisdiction of the Ombudsman. The 1993 review may be seen as representing a important step in the development of an office which, in the view of Professor Anthony Bradley, is already making 'a positive and original contribution to the improvement of public administration'.

Evidence of this contribution can be seen in the Ombudsman's investigation of maladministration in the Channel Tunnel Rail Link Development. Whereas the Department of Transport refused to accept a finding of maladministration, the government gave compensation 'out of respect for the Select Committee on the Parliamentary Commissioner and the Office of the Parliamentary Commissioner'.

Devolution

Whilst it is important to note that the Parliament at Westminster retains its sovereignty and the Act of Union remains on the statute book, significant changes have been made to our constitution via the Scotland Act 1998, the Wales Act 1998 and the Northern Ireland Act 1998.

Whereas these Acts do not promote a federal style uniform devolution of power, they do, in total, represent a fundamental redistribution of power within the UK.

Pursuant to the referendum held in September 1997, the new Scottish Parliament of 1999 has legislative power over the legal system, police and penal system, economic development, industrial assistance, education and training, and also has tax-varying powers. However, in Wales, the referendum on devolution produced a much less convincing affirmative vote and the resultant National Assembly for Wales has no tax varying power or any power to enact primary legislation. Nevertheless, it does have an executive function and under Transfer Orders will carry out the functions previously performed by the Secretary of State for Wales in the areas of:

Agriculture, forestry, fisheries and food; Ancient monuments and historic buildings; Culture (including museums, galleries and libraries; Economic development; Education and training; Environment; Health and health services; Highways; Housing, industry; Local government; Social services; Sport and recreation; Tourism; Town and country planning; Transport; Water and flood defence; The Welsh language

The Northern Ireland Act system is different again and is intended to take account of the totality of relationships within the island of Ireland. In so doing, the following new institutions will be introduced into our constitution: a Northern Ireland Assembly; North-South Ministerial Council (together with cross-border implementation bodies); British-Irish Council; and British-Irish Inter-governmental Conference.

The English dimension is addressed by a governmental commitment to directly-elected regional government in England, but only where 'a clear popular consent is established'. This would be additional to any developments stemming from directly-elected Mayor and separately elected Assembly for London and the general reform of local government referred to earlier.

3 The citizen and the executive

Power and accountability

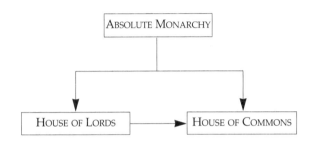

Beating at the heart of any study of constitutional law are issues of power and accountability. We are said to have a constitution based upon the concept of parliamentary sovereignty.

This means that, in contradiction to the separation of powers, we hold our legislature, as studied in Chapter 2, to be the supreme power within the state. Yet, as we will see, for many commentators, our constitution has evolved beyond this theoretical foundation to the extent that it is now not the legislature which controls the executive but rather the executive, through its domination of the party machine, which controls the legislature.

At one time during our constitutional history, the Monarch was the sovereign political power within the State through direct or in direct control of the executive, legislature and judiciary. The source of the Monarch's power was the Royal Prerogative, a term derived from the Latin *prae* (before) and

CONSTITUTIONAL LAW

rogo (I demand). Thus, the Royal Prerogative is what the Monarch demanded and was entitled to in preference to all others. The scope of the Monarch's absolute and discretionary powers became a matter for bitter dispute in Stuart times between royalist and parliamentary lawyers.

In *Bate's Case* (1606), the Barons of the Exchequer found for King James I, when Bate refused to pay a tax on imported currants, on the basis that the regulation of foreign trade was ancillary to the King's prerogative in foreign affairs. In the *Case of Prohibitions del Roy* (1607), it was noted by Chief Justice Coke that the King, 'in his own person, cannot adjudge any case, either criminal ... or between party and party ... but this ought to be determined and adjudged in some court of justice'. The *Case of Proclamations* (1611) decided that the King, 'by his proclamation or other ways, cannot change any part of the common law or statute law, or the customs of the realm ... and the King cannot create any offence by his prohibition or proclamation which was not an offence before ...'. In *Darnel's Case* (1627), the response to a writ of habeas corpus that Darnel was imprisoned by special command of the King authorised by privy council warrant was deemed sufficient for the judges. In *R v Hampden* (1637), common law judges found by majority for King Charles I when Hampden refused to pay a tax. The tax, to create a navy to defend shipping, had been authorised under the prerogative power for the defence of the realm but had not been sanctioned by Parliament. Hampden had argued that, even if the King could raise taxes without reference to Parliament, he could only do so where a real danger to the defence of the realm was proved.

The struggle between the Stuart monarchy and Parliament finally culminated in the removal of James II from the throne in the Glorious Revolution 1688 and his replacement by the Protestant William and Mary of Orange, subject to the Bill of Rights 1689. The Bill of Rights 1689 placed the concept of the sovereignty of parliament on a legal footing through the severe curtailment of the Royal Prerogative. It established as a general principle that prerogative powers can be either limited or abolished by statute.

The case of *AG v De Keyser's Royal Hotel* (1920) served to amplify this position. It was held in this case that Parliament may both expressly limit or abolish a prerogative and do so by implication. The latter is achieved by merely passing a statute which is inconsistent with the prerogative, although, in such an instance, the prerogative is only put into abeyance and presumably revives with the repeal of the statute.

Moreover, in *R v Secretary of State for the Home Department ex p Fire Brigades Union* (1995), the House of Lords affirmed the principle that the prerogative cannot be used to achieve an objective provided for by statute. Thus, compensation payments under the Criminal Justice Act 1988 could only be replaced by a subsequent legislation, in the form of the Criminal Injuries Compensation Act 1995.

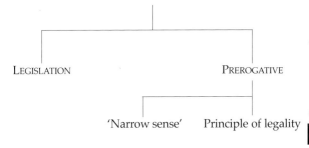

Source of executive power

In his work, *The Study of the Law of the Constitution* (1885), Professor AV Dicey concluded: '... the prerogative appears to be both historically and as a matter of fact nothing less than the residue of discretionary and arbitrary authority, which at any given time is legally left in the hands of the Crown.'

Many of these prerogative powers are today, however, not exercised by the Monarch in person but by other members of the executive in the name of the Crown. Even those prerogative powers which still remain within the personal domain of the Monarch, such as the dissolution of Parliament, the appointment of the Prime Minister, the dismissal of ministers, the granting of honours, are all constrained in their exercise by rules of convention.

Thus, under the umbrella term of 'Crown', what was once the Royal Prerogative has, in fact, become an important source of executive power. In *Council of Civil Service Unions v Minister for the Civil Service* (1985), the court followed the lead of Professor AV Dicey and used the term prerogative to cover all non-statutory actions of the executive. By contrast, in his article entitled 'The "third source" of authority for government action' (1992) LQR, BV Harris identified three *sources* of executive authority. The first source of authority is statute, giving delegated powers to ministers. The second is the prerogative, as Professor Sir William Wade would understand it, in *the narrow sense*, namely, those ancient prerogatives which the courts through the common law have recognised as being unique to the Crown. The third is, in actual fact, not a source but rather a freedom – the freedom enjoyed by the Crown to do anything not prohibited by law. This freedom is the consequence of the principle of legality, that everything is legal that is not illegal.

An illustration of the principle of legality is seen in *Malone v Metropolitan Police Commissioner* (1979). Authority for officers of the Crown to tap telephones stemmed from the fact that there is no right of privacy under our law and thus no law to prohibit the Crown tapping telephones (note the subsequent enactment of Interception of Communications Act 1985).

Crown

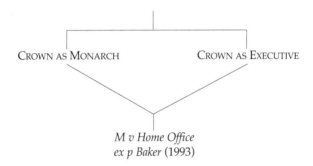

To some judges, such as Lord Diplock in *Town Investments v Department of the Environment* (1978), executive use of the Royal Prerogative was such that the reality of the situation had become that all actions of the executive were 'acts done by "the Crown" in the fictional sense in which that expression is now used in English public law'.

This position, however, caused consternation in many academic quarters. In his series of articles entitled 'The

CONSTITUTIONAL LAW

Crown – old platitudes and new heresies' (1993) NLJ, Professor Sir William Wade identified it as his first, and perhaps most important, heresy. He noted that, in terms of executive action today, the vast majority of powers 'belong to ministers, not to the Crown, and this fact, combined with the non-immunity of Crown servants, forms the bedrock on which the Rule of Law stands'. His conclusion was that, if judges allow the legal distinction between the Crown and the government, as servants of the Crown, to be removed, then the Rule of Law was itself at stake. He looked to *M v Home Office ex p Baker* (1993), 'the most important case in constitutional law for the last 200 years and more', to settle the issue.

Taking note of the fact that, 'Parliament makes the law, the executive carry the law into effect and the judiciary enforce the law', Lord Templeman held that:

> ... the expression 'the Crown' has two meanings, namely the Monarch and the executive. In the 17th century, Parliament established its supremacy over the Crown as Monarch, over the executive and over the judiciary ... parliamentary supremacy over the judiciary is only exercisable by statute. The judiciary enforce the law against individuals, against institutions and against the executive. The judges cannot enforce the law against the Crown as Monarch because the Crown as Monarch can do no wrong but judges enforce the law against the Crown as executive and against individuals who from time to time represent the Crown ... the submission that there is no power to enforce the law by injunction or contempt proceedings against a minister in his official capacity would, if upheld, establish the proposition that the executive obey the law as a matter of grace and not as

a matter of necessity, a proposition which would reverse the result of the civil war.

Lord Templeman was not prepared to follow the finding of Simon Brown J at first instance that, 'when it comes to the enforcement of its decisions, the relationship between the executive and the judiciary must, in the end, be one of trust'.

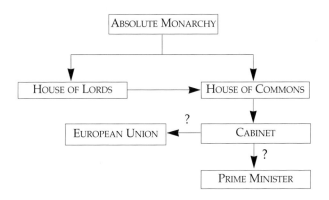

Prime ministerial government?

In his introduction to *The English Constitution* by Walter Bagehot in 1963, Richard Crossman confidently asserted that 'the post-war epoch has seen the final transformation of cabinet government into prime ministerial government'. But, was his confidence justified?

Certainly, Lord Hailsham believed it was when he delivered The Dimbleby Lecture in 1972. In his lecture entitled 'Elective Dictatorship', Lord Hailsham traced the movement of power within our constitution from medieval monarchy to modern democracy and noted:

Until comparatively recently, Parliament consisted of two effective chambers. Now, for most practical purposes, it consists of one. Until recently, the powers of government within Parliament were largely controlled either by the opposition or by its own backbenchers. It is now largely in the hands of the government machine, so that the government controls Parliament and not Parliament the government ... So, the sovereignty of Parliament has increasingly become, in practice, the sovereignty of the Commons, and the sovereignty of the Commons has increasingly become the sovereignty of the government, which, in addition to its influence in Parliament, controls the party whips, the party machine, and the civil service.

This led Lord Hailsham to conclude that 'we live under an elective dictatorship, absolute in theory, if hitherto thought tolerable in practice'. But, what evidence is there to justify such a conclusion?

Certainly, few could doubt the growth of cabinet government. The origins of cabinet government lie in the late 17th century and the creation, by Charles II, of a small *cabal* of privy counsellors in order to alleviate the frustration of working through the full Privy Council. Thus, far from being created by statute the Cabinet, as an institution, merely evolved out of the Privy Council and is still technically one of its committees.

At this time, the members of the Cabinet were important court officials and not responsible to Parliament. However, in the 18th century, parliamentary power steadily increased and it became politically expedient for the Monarch to choose as close advisers politicians with sufficient influence to secure the passage of measures, and especially financial measures, through the legislature.

By the time of the Reform Acts of 1832 and 1867, the power of the Monarch to appoint ministers without taking the advice of leading parliamentary figures was effectively lost. With the expansion in the electorate came a growth in party politics. The Cabinet then began to emerge as the dominant political body within the constitution, representing in government the collective leadership of the party which was able to command a majority in the House of Commons.

From this growing dominance of the Cabinet emerged two new conventions of the constitution which are crucial to the working of modern Cabinet government. The first is that ministers of the Crown are accountable, both collectively and individually, to Parliament; the second, that the Crown must only act as ministers advise it to act.

Out of the prominent party figures within the Cabinet, however, a leading figure would inevitably be recognised. It is from this that the office of the Prime Minister evolved. Thus, as with the Cabinet, the office of Prime Minister originated as a *de facto* (in fact) institution as opposed to one created *de jure* (in law). It exists by convention of the constitution and its powers are similarly only defined by convention.

Originally acknowledged as being merely *primus inter pares* (first amongst equals) and associated with the position of First Lord of the Treasury, the office has continued to grow in constitutional importance. Indeed, in his book, *The Hidden Wiring: Unearthing the British Constitution* (1995), Professor Peter Hennessy argues that virtually the whole weight of governing our state has passed to the shoulders of the Prime

Minister, with only limited support from the Cabinet on the one side and the Monarch on the other.

Some commentators would see the Thatcher premiership as providing this final transition into prime ministerial government. Writing in the *Guardian* newspaper in November 1988, Richard Holmes, editor of the Constitutional Reform Centre, warned that we now had a constitution in shambles:

> ... as government presses on towards the very limits of partisanship, the frail conventions which once provided at least the illusion of consent to cover the naked exercise of power, have one by one been ripped away.

In his book entitled *Thatcherism and British Politics: the End of Consensus* (1990), Professor Kavanagh concluded that 'it is very difficult to imagine a Prime Minister in good health being deposed by cabinet colleagues'.

Yet, for many, the role of the Cabinet in Lady Thatcher's removal from power had been crucial and demanded a reassessment of the importance of the Cabinet. In his article, 'The end of prime ministerial government?' (1991) PL 1, Professor Geoffrey Marshall went further by stating:

> ... given that British prime ministers, unlike American presidents, are so obviously dependent upon the continued support of their party majorities and Cabinet colleagues, one might wonder how it could ever have come to be plausibly asserted that 'the post-war epoch has seen the final transformation of cabinet government into prime ministerial government'.

Ministerial responsibility

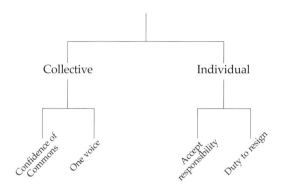

Collective responsibility

It is one of the central features of our evolutionary constitution that Parliament, through the concept of its own supremacy and corresponding reduction in the powers of the Monarch, has been able to assert the accountability of the government as a whole to Parliament. This collective responsibility owed to Parliament takes two forms.

First, the government must resign if it loses the support of the elected chamber. An example of this would be the resignation of James Callaghan (now Lord Callaghan) government in 1979 and the consequent general election. Understanding this part of the convention is crucial to an appreciation of its significance to the operation of our constitution. It goes to the very heart of the relationship between our legislature and executive. Yet, this is not to say that the convention is a major constitutional constraint on executive power. It can actually serve to strengthen the position of the executive. Thus, when John Major and his Cabinet suffered a defeat by 324 votes to 316 in Parliament on 22 July 1992 (largely at the hands of 23 backbench rebels) on a motion relating to the Maastricht Treaty on European Union, he was able to restore his authority by putting down a motion of confidence for the following day. The motion inevitably secured a majority as the rebels within his party knew that its defeat would have led to the dissolution of Parliament and the possibility of the Labour party winning the subsequent general election.

The second form collective responsibility takes can also serve to enhance the position of the Prime Minister. If government is to be made accountable to Parliament, then the action for which it is held to be responsible must be clear. Such clarity can only be achieved by the government speaking with but one voice. This part of the convention has a crucial bearing on the operation of the Cabinet.

By convention, civil service advice to cabinet ministers is confidential, as is the ensuing discussion between ministers themselves. But, whatever the advice or discussion, once the government's position has been made clear, all members of the Cabinet are held collectively responsible for it. Thus, a minister in the minority opinion in cabinet has but three options: either to accept and publicly defend the decision; tender their resignation or seek to breach the convention by secretly briefing the media on their disquiet with government policy.

However, the political reality of a given situation can cause even a Prime Minister to give ground. For example, to avoid the possibility of mass resignation and the political embarrassment it would cause, Harold Wilson once waived the operation of this part of the convention. It should be noted, however, that this *agreement to differ* amongst cabinet colleagues only related to the issue of continuing membership of the common market and the convention was fully restored after the referendum in 1975.

Individual responsibility

One of the important features of our civil service is its claim to political neutrality. Civil servants are meant to remain as the anonymous advisers of government ministers. It is felt that without such anonymity their position of permanency within our constitution would be threatened.

Thus, a minister is expected to accept a responsibility for the protection of their civil servant advisers. This means that a minister is not only responsible to Parliament in a collective sense for the policies of the government as a whole but is also responsible in an individual sense for their own actions and those of their department. But, are ministers constitutionally accountable to Parliament for every action undertaken by their civil servants?

This question was central to what has become known as the 'Crichel Down affair'. In 1939, the Air Ministry compulsorily acquired Crichel Down, an area of farmland in Dorset. After the Second World War, the land was transferred to the Ministry of Agriculture who refused a request from the previous owners to re-purchase it. This refusal was accompanied by misleading replies and the matter was taken up in Parliament. Following an inquiry which found 'inefficiency, bias and bad faith' on the part of some officials, five of whom were named, the minister, Sir Thomas Dugdale, resigned.

The most important constitutional aspect in this affair is the subsequent statement by the Home Secretary, Sir David Maxwell-Fyfe in the House of Commons, on when a minister must accept responsibility for the actions of their civil servants. The Home Secretary made clear that such a constitutional duty existed where the civil servant was carrying out either government policy or the explicit orders of the minister. If a civil servant caused delay or makes a mistake, but not on a major issue of policy or not where individual rights are seriously affected, the minister must again acknowledge responsibility and ensure that corrective action is taken within the department. The minister was deemed not to be under such a constitutional duty where, otherwise than above, the minister had no previous knowledge and disapproved of the action taken by the civil servant. This leads us to the second issue of, having accepted responsibility for the actions of their civil servants, when is a minister under an obligation to resign?

It is, perhaps, much to the credit of our civil service that the vast majority of ministerial resignations in the last dozen years have resulted from the actions of ministers and cabinet colleagues rather than their civil servants.

However, issues of accountability have come to the fore in the academic debate on dramatic organisational changes to the structure and running of our civil service. In the parliamentary session 1987–88, the Treasury and Civil Service Select Committee reported that changes proposed to the civil service by the efficiency unit 'could be the most far reaching since the Northcote-Trevelyan Reforms in the 19th century'.

Originally led by Lord Rayner, the efficiency unit, by the time of Mrs Thatcher's third successive election victory in

1987, was now under the control of Sir Robin Ibbs. The Ibbs proposal was that the devolved budgeting principles inherent in the Financial Management Initiative, introduced by his predecessor in 1982, should be followed up in 1988 with the launch of *Improving Management in Government: The Next Steps Initiative.*

The basis of the proposal was that 95% of civil service activity was concerned with public service delivery, which could be provided more effectively by 'hiving-off' such administrative functions to new executive agencies. The Fulton Report of 1968 had also given a cautious welcome to the possibility of 'hiving-off' but, by 1977, the old Expenditure Committee was warning that it was 'only viable in limited areas of government ... and should be approached with caution ... hiving-off necessarily involves a diminution in the area of ministerial control'.

Ten years on, such concerns were put to one side when the then Prime Minister, Margaret Thatcher, announced the appointment of Peter Kemp to the Office of the Minister for the Civil Service as project officer overseeing the implementation of the Next Steps Initiative. The committed aim was to:

> ... establish a quite different way of conducting the business of government. The central Civil Service should consist of a relatively small core engaged in the function of servicing ministers and managing departments, who will be the 'sponsors' of particular government policies and services. Responding to these departments will be a range of agencies employing their own staff ... and concentrating on the delivery of their particular service.

When pressed on the point by Terence Higgins, chairman of the Treasury and Civil Service Committee, the Prime Minister sought to reassure that there would be 'no change in the arrangements for accountability'. Yet, in a series of articles on this issue, Professor Gavin Drewry poses the fundamental question:

> ... how can ministers credibly cling to their virtual monopoly of accountability to Parliament, via traditional models of ministerial responsibility that (according to the Prime Minister) are to remain unaltered by 'The Next Steps', in respect of semi-autonomous agencies whose chief executives are expected to take managerial initiatives at arm's length from ministerial control?

The significance of the question became all the more apparent in 1995 when, following the removal of Derek Lewis (its Director General), the Home Secretary, Michael Howard, refused to accept individual responsibility for the running of the prison service. Michael Howard sought to separate *policy* considerations from *operational* matters, which he contended were the sole responsibility of the Prisons Board.

4 The citizen and judicial control of the abuse of power

What is judicial review?

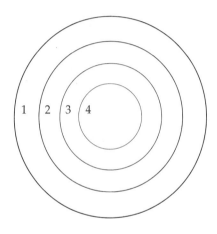

	4	Judicial review
within	3	Administrative law
within	2	Constitutional law
within	1	Public law

No study of constitutional law would be complete without a study of administrative law. Yet, the definition and scope of both, together with public law in general, is open to interpretation.

The distinction between public law and private law is fundamental to many legal systems and in particular those whose origins lie in Roman law. Public law is that body of law which directly relates to the state and its relationship with its citizens. The body of private law within a State regulates the relationships between its citizens.

Administrative law can be said to contain the body of general principles which govern the exercise of powers and duties by public bodies. Further, that it is the law relating to the control of governmental power'.

Administrative law therefore addresses public law issues. But so to does constitutional law so what, if any, difference is there between them? Professor Sir William Wade stated in *Administrative Law* (1988) that:

> ... the whole of administrative law ... may be treated as a branch of constitutional law, since it flows directly from the constitutional principles of the Rule of Law, the sovereignty of Parliament and the independence of the judiciary; and it does much to determine the balance of power between the State and the citizen.

A detailed study of administrative law would require a consideration of administrative rules and procedures, the work of administrative tribunals and inquiries and the ombudsman system. But, at the core of any study of administrative law lies judicial review.

Judicial review relates to the granting of the prerogative orders of certiorari, mandamus and prohibition. These prerogative powers were historically used by the Council of the King to supervise the work of justices of the peace who had both judicial and administrative responsibilities within localities.

With the growth of the administrative State, these supervisory powers, which were now in the hands of judges of the Queen's Bench Division, started to acquire ever increasing importance. By 1929, Lord Chief Justice Hewart was beginning to express judicial concern at 'the new despotism'. In particular, there was increasing unease with the growth of delegated legislation and the wide discretionary powers Parliament was granting to ministers. Such concern ultimately led to an investigation by the Donoughmore-Scott Committee on ministers' powers.

A good illustration of the powers now being conferred on ministers by Parliament is found in the Deregulation and Contracting Out Act 1994, which allows for the suspension of any provision of any Act if the minister believes it to impose an unnecessary burden on trade. Thus, whereas citizens are asked to accept delegated legislation as a necessary evil, it is recognised that the judiciary have an important role to play in ensuring that an ever powerful executive at least acts within its powers.

What bodies are subject to judicial review?

Body	Decision	Procedure	Remedies	Grounds
			Mandamus	1 Illegality
	Public	Order 53	*Certiorari*	2 Procedural
			Prohibition	Impropriety
				3 Irrationality
Public				
	Private	Writ		
	Private	Writ		
Private				
	Public	Order 53		

The fundamental question of what bodies are subject to judicial review is in such a state of present confusion and uncertainty so as to render it a prime area for a question in the examination. Judicial use of the prerogative orders of *mandamus, certiorari* and prohibition is discretionary and it is the judges themselves who have set the limitations and direction of judicial review.

In 1923, Atkin LJ held in *R v Electricity Commissioners ex p London Electricity Joint Committee* (1924) that 'any body of persons having legal authority to determine questions affecting the rights of subjects, and having the duty to act judicially ...' were susceptible to an application for a judicial review. By 1964, the legal distinction between having a duty to act judicially, as opposed to a mere administrative duty, was effectively removed by Lord Reid in *Ridge v Baldwin* (1964).

The next development occurred three years later in 1967. Up until that time, judicial review was confined to those inferior bodies to which Parliament had delegated powers (*vires*). It was the task of the court, through judicial review, to ensure that these inferior bodies operated within their powers (*intra vires*) and did not go beyond either the express or implied limits of their power (*ultra vires*). The implied limits on their power were set by judges and known as the '*Wednesbury* principles' (*Associated Provincial Picture Houses v Wednesbury Corpn* (1948)).

In *R v Criminal Injuries Board ex p Lain* (1967), however, judicial review was extended to include bodies acting pursuant to prerogative powers. This development was affirmed by judges of the House of Lords in *Council of Civil Service Unions v Minister for the Civil Service* (1985). Although the court went on to identify areas relating to the prerogative where judicial review would not be used ('the making of treaties; the defence of the realm; the prerogative of mercy; the grant of honours; the dissolution of Parliament and the appointment of ministers ...'), it was subsequently decided by Watkins LJ in *R v Home Secretary ex p Bentley* (1993) that the prerogative of mercy was subject to judicial review and 'it will be for other courts to decide on a case by case basis whether (other aspects are) reviewable or not ...'.

Thus, judges no longer confine the jurisdiction of judicial review of inferior bodies acting outside their *vires*. Instead, we are told by Lord Templeman in *R v ITC ex p TSW Broadcasting* (1992) that judges 'invented the remedy of judicial review ... to ensure that the decision maker did not (either) exceed or abuse his powers'. But, the question still remains, which decision makers are susceptible to an application for a judicial review?

R v Panel on Takeovers and Mergers ex p Datafin (1987) represents a major development for it was recognised by the judges that the panel had 'no statutory, prerogative or common law powers' and so performed its functions 'without visible means of legal support'. We may therefore say that decision makers acting under statutory powers are subject to judicial review, as are decision makers acting under prerogative powers, subject to certain limitations. But, according to *R v Panel on Takeovers and Mergers ex p Datafin* (1987), so too is any decision maker subject to the nature of their decision. This blurring of the significance of the type of body taking the decision may be controversial but is growing in importance when one considers the recent government policy of taking bodies out of the public sector for the intended purpose of efficiency gain.

We have already noted that, since the 1980s, we have seen a revolution in the administration of many sectors of government activity. The civil service has undergone a programme of radical reform with the *Next Steps Initiative* and the growth of 'executive agencies' (for example, Driver Vehicle Licensing Agency; United Kingdom Passport Agency). The National Health Service is undergoing major managerial reform with the National Health Service and Community Care Act 1990 and 'trust status hospitals'. The function of local authorities has been transformed. Local education authority colleges in the further and higher education sector have been given 'corporate status'. Most publicly owned corporations have been 'privatised' (for example, British Telecom and all the utilities, such as electricity, gas and water). Many of these privatised industries have had 'regulatory agencies' imposed upon them, such as OFTEL (telephones); OFFER (electricity); OFGAS (gas); OFWAT (water). These new bodies join other regulatory agencies prescribed by statute or prerogative, such as the Civil Aviation Authority; Commission for Racial Equality; Equal Opportunities Commission; Independent Television Commission; Monopolies and Mergers Commission; the Welsh Development Agency, etc, all variously described as *quangos* (quasi-autonomous non-governmental bodies); fringe bodies or non-departmental public bodies. In addition to these prescribed regulatory bodies, there are voluntary or self-regulatory agencies, such as the Panel on Takeovers and Mergers; the Advertising Standards Authority and various sporting bodies, such as the Jockey Club and Football Association.

What decisions are subject to judicial review?

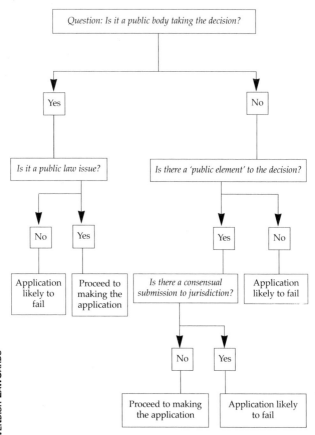

In the view of Sir John Donaldson, the then Master of the Rolls, in *R v Panel on Takeovers and Mergers ex p Datafin* (1987), it is clear that:

> ... the only essential elements are what can be described as a public element ... and the exclusion [of] ... a consensual submission to ... jurisdiction.

It is clear from *R v East Berkshire Health Authority ex p Walsh* (1985) and *R v Chief Rabbi ex p Wachmann* (1992) that the requirement of the decision having a public element is not satisfied simply because the public is interested in the result. Justice Simon Brown said in the latter case:

> ... whether a decision has public law consequences must be determined otherwise than by reference to the seriousness of its impact upon those affected.

It would also be wrong to assume that just because the decision maker is a public body, namely, a body created by royal prerogative, statute or statutory instrument, that all its decisions are subject to judicial review. In *R v BBC ex p Lavelle* (1983) and *R v East Berkshire Health Authority ex p Walsh* (1985), the decisions of these public bodies were not susceptible to a judicial review because they related to employment matters within the private law domain. Likewise, *R v IBA ex p Rank* (1986) and *R v NCB ex p NUM* (1986) where commercial decisions were not held to be reviewable.

In *R v Panel on Takeovers and Mergers ex p Datafin* (1985), Lloyd LJ states that '... the source of the power will often, perhaps usually, be decisive'. The decisions of public bodies acting under statutory or prerogative authority are likely, therefore, to be presumed by judges to have a public element unless it can be proved to the contrary. But, what of non-public bodies?

Here, judges have adopted a simple '*but for*' test. But for the existence of that non-public body, would the State be likely to enact legislation to confer statutory powers on a comparable body to regulate the area of life over which the non-public body has *de facto* control?

In *R v Chief Rabbi ex p Wachmann* (1992), Simon Brown J concluded that the decisions of the Chief Rabbi were not subject to judicial review because:

> ... his functions are essentially intimate, spiritual and religious, functions which the government could not and would not seek to discharge in his place were he to abdicate his regulatory responsibility.

It is an well established principle that judicial review cannot be used to regulate the decisions of bodies with which the applicant has voluntarily entered into a consensual (contractual) relationship. In his article, 'Who is subject to judicial review and in respect of what?' (1992) PL, David Pannick argues that this principle has been misapplied by judges in some of the applications involving sporting bodies. In his article 'Pitch, pool, rink ... court? Judicial review in the sporting world' (1989) PL, Michael Beloff believes it is:

> ... the floodgates argument that is the unspoken premise of precedents relating to sporting bodies ... the fear that limited court time will be absorbed by a new and elastic category of case with much scope for abusive or captious litigation.

For Michael Beloff:

> ... it is an argument which intellectually has little to commend it and pragmatically is usually shown to be ill founded.

It is suggested by David Pannick that the better course is to follow the views expressed by Simon Brown J in *R v Chief Rabbi ex p Wachmann* (1992) where he rejected the argument that the Chief Rabbi is not subject to judicial review because 'no one is compelled to be a Jew, or Orthodox Jew, still less a Rabbi', for as he explained:

> ... an Orthodox Rabbi is pursuing a vocation and has no choice but to accept the Chief Rabbi's disciplinary decisions.

One might argue, therefore, that judicial review should not be excluded for reasons of *consensual submission* where the relevant body has monopolistic powers which the applicant has to accept if they wish to participate in the area of life governed by the body in question.

The procedure for making an application for a judicial review

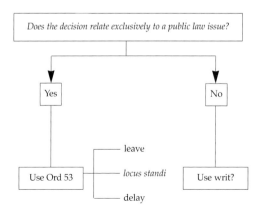

The initial concern of any litigant in administrative law is which procedure should be adopted to commence proceedings. In essence, the two types of procedure reflect the public law and private law divide. An application for a judicial review will have the High Court as the court of first instance. Thus, the procedure to be adopted is prescribed in the *Rules of the Supreme Court* (White Book). In particular, Ord 53 contains the rules relating to a judicial review application.

Up until 1977, this procedure did not allow for cross-examination on affidavits; discovery; interrogatories and the private law remedies of damages; declaration or injunction to be added to the claim for the prerogative orders of mandamus, certiorari and prohibition. Responding to the Law Commission report, *Remedies in Administrative Law* (1976), these deficiencies were removed by *Rules of the Supreme Court (Amendment No 3) 1977* (SI 1977/1955).

In particular, Ord 53 r 7 allows a claim for damages if damages would have been available in an action started by writ, and Ord 53 r 8 allows for the discovery of documents, administering of interrogatories and cross-examination of deponents on affidavits. These procedural reforms were later enshrined in s 31 of the Supreme Court Act 1981.

The other procedural obstacles remained. The justification being that the courts needed greater control over public law proceedings than private law proceedings, that the essence of the public law proceeding was speed and that it was important to channel these actions to the specialist judges assigned to the crown office list.

Order 53 r 3 requires the obtaining of leave of the court. Order 53 r 3(7) only allows leave to be granted where the applicant has a sufficient interest, known by the Latin tag *locus standi*. The leading decision of *R v IRC ex p National Federation of Self-Employed and Small Businesses* (1982) establishes that the issue of sufficient interest may be considered at both the leave stage and at the hearing. Order 53 r 4 requires that an application:

> ... shall be made promptly and, in any event, within three months from the date when grounds for the application first arose unless the court considers that there is good reason for extending the period.

This is not to say, however, that Ord 53 r 4 offers a three month limitation period. It was made equally clear by judges in the High Court in *R v Swale BC ex p RSPB* (1990) that an application for a judicial review can be struck out on the grounds of undue delay even when it is initiated within a three month period.

By contrast, private law actions against public bodies are commenced by ordinary writ issued in the plaintiff's own name. Little wonder that there was and still remains a preference for applicants to use this procedure. However, in the important decision of the House of Lords in *O'Reilly v Mackman* (1983), it was held to be an abuse of the process of court to allow an action to continue by way of writ when it should rightly have been commenced under the Ord 53 procedure with all its constraints. Lord Diplock concluded that the reasons justifying the avoidance of Ord 53 had now been removed with the procedural reforms of 1977 and there were sound policy reasons justifying the insistence that an applicant overcome the Ord 53 safeguards. Nevertheless, Lord Diplock recognised that there would be exceptions to this general rule:

... particularly where the invalidity of the decision arises as a collateral issue in a claim ... under private law, or where none of the parties objects to ... procedure by writ.

The severity of this general rule became the cause of much academic debate and, in *Roy v Kensington Family Practitioner Committee* (1992), Lord Lowry set about defusing the 'procedural minefield' laid by Lord Diplock. With the support of his colleague Lord Bridge, he made it clear that in his view *O'Reilly v Mackman* (1983) should be given a limited interpretation, so as not to create a general rule that all challenges to public law decisions had to follow the Order 53 procedure. In *The Trustees of the Dennis Rye Pension Fund v Sheffield City Council* (1998), the Court of Appeal ruled that courts should not be overly concerned with the distinction, but should look to the practical consequences of pursuing the alternative actions.

Procedural reforms

| JUSTICE/ALL SOULS | REMEDIES IN ADMINISTRATIVE LAW (1976) | JUDICIAL REVIEW AND STATUTORY APPEALS (1994) |

In the 1960s, a series of seminars were held in All Souls College, Oxford by the Law Commission to investigate procedural and other defects in our public law. The Law Commission recommended the establishment of a royal commission to investigate the matter. The failure of successive governments to take action ultimately led to the formation of an unofficial body of investigation. To quote from its report:

> ... in 1978, a committee was formed under the auspices of JUSTICE (the British section of the International Commission of Jurists) and All Souls College, Oxford, to under take a full scale examination of administrative law in the United Kingdom.

It was against this background of an on-going review that the Law Commission made its report, *Remedies in Administrative Law* (1976), which led to the reform of Ord 53 in 1977 and the passing of s 31 of the Supreme Court Act 1981. In his important contribution to the debate, 'Judicial review: a possible programme for reform' (1992) PL, Sir Harry Woolf expressed his deep concern as to state and future of judicial review. Such progress as there had been in the 1980s:

> ... was only possible because of the procedural reforms (cited above) ... they provided a structure within which the developments could take place.

Lord Woolf continued with his theme by stating:

> The former Lord Chief Justice (Lord Lane) has compared that structure with a motorway and pointed out that, if you provide motorway, it will become an invitation for the public to respond by using it. This, in the case of judicial review, has proved all too true. There is a danger of it becoming as overcrowded as the M25. The tailback, or backlogs, are becoming more and more disturbing. The use of judicial review has grown and is continuing to grow at a pace with which the present structure cannot cope ... What is more, I believe that the rate of increase, far from slowing down, is going to accelerate.

Many of the proposals made by Lord Woolf for further procedural reform have been considered by the Law Commission in its most recent paper, *Administrative Law: Judicial Review and Statutory Appeals* (1994). Whereas media attention has tended to focus on the recommendation to simplify the title of the remedies from mandamus, certiorari and prohibition to mandatory, restraining and quashing orders, it is the areas of leave and *locus standi* (standing) which contain the most interesting proposals. The Law Commission would recommend re-naming leave 'preliminary consideration' and suggests the test that the applicant discloses 'a serious issue', rather than the present test of showing 'an arguable case'. Judges would make a 'request for information' from respondents and would be required to give reasons for refusing leave. The area of *locus standi* has already undergone considerable development, from the reluctance of judges to allow a public interest challenge in *R v Secretary of State for the Environment ex p Rose Theatre Trust* (1990), to allowing standing for Greenpeace in *R v Inspectorate of Pollution ex p Greenpeace* (1994), the Equal Opportunities Commission in *R v Secretary of State for Employment ex p Equal Opportunities Commission* (1994) and the World Development Movement in *R v Secretary of State for Foreign and Commonwealth Affairs ex p World Development Movement* (1994). The Law Commission would envisage a two-track system of standing in judicial review proceedings. Individual applicants with 'legal personality' would continue to have standing, but only in matters where they have been 'personally adversely affected' by the decision. In public interest challenges, the Law Commission would recommend a 'broad discretion' as to standing, and a corresponding amendment to s 31(4)(b) of the Supreme Court Act 1981.

Professor Richard Gordon noted:

> ... case load management philosophy looms large in the Commission's proposals, especially in respect of the leave stage. So, too, does the creation of a new public interest focus. The two philosophies are not necessarily mutually exclusive but they are hardly complimentary.

Grounds for judicial review

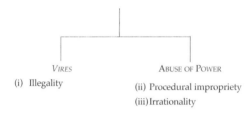

VIRES

(i) Illegality

ABUSE OF POWER

(ii) Procedural impropriety

(iii) Irrationality

Two stages

Up until 1984, textbooks traditionally defined the grounds for judicial review as being *ultra vires* caused by the breach of a rule of natural justice; or caused by the failure to follow a procedural requirement prescribed by statute; or caused by a body acting in excess of its legal jurisdiction or abusing its powers by acting in contravention of the '*Wednesbury* principles'. The only exception was a grounds for review, revived in *R v Northumberland Compensation Appeal Tribunal ex p Shaw* (1952) of 'error of law on the face of the record'. This was an exception because the body was acting within its jurisdiction when taking the decision (that is, *intra vires*) but the decision had been reached via an erroneous interpretation of the law recorded in its proceedings.

The categorisation of the grounds of review changed, however, with the judgment of Lord Diplock in the leading case of *Council of Civil Service Unions v Minister for the Civil Service* (1985):

> Judicial review has, I think, developed to a stage today when, without reiterating any analysis of the steps by which the development has come about, one can conveniently classify under three heads the grounds upon which administrative action is subject to control by judicial review. The first ground I would call 'illegality', the second 'irrationality' and the third 'procedural impropriety'. That is not to say that further development on a case by case basis may not in the course of time add further grounds ... By 'illegality' as a ground for judicial review, I mean that the decision maker must understand correctly the law that regulates his decision making power and must give effect to it. Whether he has or not is *par excellence* a justiciable question to be decided, in the event of dispute, by those persons, the judges, by whom the judicial power of state is exercisable. By 'irrationality', I mean what can by now be succinctly referred to as '*Wednesbury* unreasonableness' ... It applies to a decision which is so outrageous in its defiance of logic or of accepted moral standards that no sensible person who had applied his mind to the question to be decided could have arrived at it ... I have described the third head as 'procedural impropriety' rather than failure to observe basic rules of natural justice ... because ... this head covers failure by an administrative tribunal to observe procedural rules that are expressly laid down in the legislative instrument by which its jurisdiction is conferred, even

where such failure does not involve any denial of natural justice.

In her article, 'Is the *ultra vires* rule the basis of judicial review?' [1987] PL 543, Professor Dawn Oliver concluded that when exercising their supervisory jurisdiction judges first concern themselves with the question of whether the decision maker was acting within their *vires* (illegality). If the answer to this question is in the affirmative, then the judge will turn to the next question of whether it can be made out that the decision maker was abusing their power (procedural impropriety and irrationality).

Vires

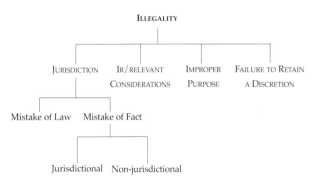

Jurisdiction

A decision maker has no *vires* and has therefore acted with illegality if they had no jurisdiction to make the decision. This can arise because the decision maker erroneously believed that they had a power to take a decision when this was not the case.

Such a mistake on the part of a decision maker is said by Lord Diplock to be *par excellence* justifiable (that is, capable of review by a judge). The judge will determine whether there has been a mistake of fact or a mistake of law. But, how does a judge distinguish between questions of fact and questions of law?

In his article, 'Mistake of fact in administrative law' (1990) PL, Timothy Jones states , 'in simple terms, one can say that a fact is a quality or event occurring at a definite place and time'. In contrast, 'law is expressed in distinctive propositions' (Hall, *General Principles of Criminal Law* (1960)). Thus:

> ... that A has killed P is a fact; the conclusion that this constitutes the crime of murder (rather than being, say, an accidental or justifiable killing) can be reached only through the application of certain propositions of law.

If the judge decides that there has been a mistake of law, then *Anisminic v Foreign Compensation Commission* (1969) would lead us to conclude that all mistakes of law go to the decision makers jurisdiction. If, however, the judge is of the opinion that there has been a mistake of fact, as opposed to a mistake of law, then the question will arise whether it is a mistake of fact which goes to the jurisdiction of the decision maker or not. Whereas mistakes of jurisdictional fact are capable of review, it would appear that a judge will not hold a non-jurisdictional mistake to be capable of review (unless the error is so excessive as to render the decision unreasonable or that there is no evidence or insufficient evidence of the existence of facts which are required to exist before the decision could have been made). The cases of *Pepper v Hart* (1993) and *Three Rivers DC v Bank of England*

(1996) illustrate the use to be made of *Hansard* to ensure decision makers remain within the intended jurisdiction of a statute.

Ir/relevant considerations

A decision maker can also be said to have acted with illegality when, in arriving at their decision, they fail to take into account things they should have taken into account and conversely do take into account things they should not have. Thus, in *R v Somerset CC ex p Fewings* (1995), the decision of the local authority was reviewable because in reaching the decision to impose a ban on hunting on ethical grounds, councillors had failed to consider whether such a ban was imposed for the 'benefit, improvement or development' of the land pursuant to s 122(1) of the Local Government Act 1972.

Improper purpose

A decision maker can be said to have acted with illegality if the decision making power is used for a purpose for which it was never intended. Thus, in *Wheeler v Leicester CC* (1985), the local authority were found to have used their powers improperly against Leicester (Rugby) Football Club when it denied the club facilities for training and playing as a punishment. The council wanted to punish the club because it was opposed to the club's attitude to sporting links with South Africa (then governed under laws of apartheid).

Failure to retain a discretion

A decision maker may also have acted with illegality if they fail to retain their decision making power. A decision maker may fail to retain their decision making power in one of two ways. First, they might delegate the decision making power

CONSTITUTIONAL LAW

75

to someone else. In *Carltona v Commissioner of Works* (1943), Lord Greene MR found it to be acceptable for a senior official to sign the actual notice requisiting a factory in time of war, even though the power of requisition had been given to a body headed by a Minister, on the basis that the Minister was accountable for the actions of the Civil Servant under the convention of ministerial responsibility. Nevertheless, *R v Home Secretary ex p Oladehinde* (1990) illustrates the limitations placed on delegation, even where the convention of ministerial responsibility is found to apply.

Secondly, a decision maker may fail to retain their decision making power when they fetter their discretion via an overly-rigid application of policy. Thus, in *British Oxygen Co Ltd v Minister of Technology* (1971), the House of Lords held that the company had not acted with inflexibility by adopting a policy because they were prepared to make exceptions to their policy on applications involving 'novel' features. Likewise, in *R v Chief Constable of North Wales Policy ex p AB* (1998), the police were found not to have adopted a policy of blanket disclosure to the public concerning the presence of a former paedophile offender, but had carefully considered the case for disclosure on its individual merit.

Abuse of power

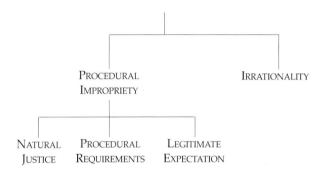

Procedural impropriety

Lord Diplock's grounds for review because of procedural impropriety can be established by persuading the judge that, whatever the merits of the decision, when arriving at the decision, the decision maker has breached a rule of natural justice, and/or had failed to adhere to a procedural requirement prescribed in the statute giving the power and/or has breached a legitimate expectation of the decision maker.

Natural justice

The three rules of natural justice are

- *audi alteram partem* (no man to be condemned without a hearing);

- *nemo judex in causa sua* (no man to be a judge in his own cause);

- a general duty for a decision maker to act fairly (although the existence of this duty is sometimes called into question).

'No man to be condemned without a hearing' usually necessitates the decision maker giving the perspective recipient of a decision adequate notice that a decision may be made and the opportunity to make representations prior to the decision being made. However, this need not necessarily mean an ability to make oral representations via a legal representative. The cases of *Glynn v Keele University* (1971) and *Cinnamond v British Airways Authority* (1980) illustrate the discretionary nature of judicial review and restrictions which judges can place upon the operation of these rules.

The rule 'no man to be a judge in his own cause' is taken to require that adjudicators must not have (or be seen to have) a pecuniary, family or professional interest in the outcome. Neither must they be otherwise biased toward the outcome, lest the impartiality of the process be questioned. We have already seen in *Re Pinochet Ugarte* (1999), following *R v Evans ex p Pinochet Ugarte; R v Bartle ex p Pinochet Ugarte; Amnesty International intervening* (1999) that whereas Lord Hoffmann had no financial or pecuniary interest in the outcome of the adjudication, the nature of his relationship with Amnesty International called into question the integrity of the adjudicatory process. This resulted in the unprecedented step of the House of Lords setting aside its earlier decision.

In *R v Gough* (1993), it was held that if 'actual bias' cannot be proved against a decision maker, it is sufficient to disclose a 'real danger' of bias. In *R v Inner West London Coroner ex p*

Pellagio (1994), a 'real danger' of bias is taken to mean more than a minimal risk of bias, if less than a probability of bias.

Judicial application of the rules of natural justice will, however, in large part be determined by the effect of a decision upon its recipient. Thus, in *McInnes v Onslow-Fame* (1978), the level of adherence to the rules of natural justice required of the decision maker was said to vary according to whether it was a forfeiture of an existing licence situation, as opposed to a mere first time application. In similar fashion, adherence to the rules of natural justice is likely to be stricter in judicial type decisions as opposed to mere administrative decisions, because the effect of the decision on the recipient is far greater.

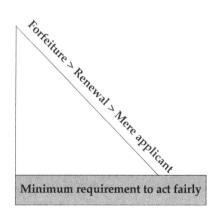

Level of Natural Justice

Forfeiture > Renewal > Mere applicant

Minimum requirement to act fairly

Type of decision

Procedural requirements

Some statutes prescribe a process a decision maker is required to undertake prior to exercising such a statutory power. Usually, this will take the form of requiring the decision maker to consult with interested parties before making a decision.

In such instances, a judge may hold that the procedural requirement prescribed in the statute is a mandatory requirement placed upon the decision maker, requiring strict and genuine observance. Thus, in *Agricultural, Horticultural and Forestry Industry Training Board v Aylesbury Mushrooms Ltd* (1972), the 'consultation' required under the Industrial Training Act 1964 was held to be more than the mere sending of a letter. There had to be 'a genuine invitation, extended with a receptive mind'.

Nevertheless, judges may introduce flexibility into the observance of statutory procedures by holding them to be merely 'directory' in nature.

Legitimate expectation

A decision maker might 'legitimately' be expected to act in a specific way before arriving at a decision, either as a result of an express promise or arising from regular past practice. Thus, in *R v Liverpool Corporate ex p Liverpool Taxi Fleet Operators Association* (1972), the council were held to be bound by a public undertaking given by a committee chairman not to increase the number of taxi licences until a Private Bill had come into force.

In *R v Council for Civil Service v Minister for the Civil Service* (1985) (the *GCHQ* case), the House of Lords recognised the legitimate expectation of the Union to be consulted prior to

Prime Minister deciding to ban membership of trade unions at GCHQ. Nevertheless, this was held to have been overridden by the issues of national security involved.

A breach of natural justice will only give rise to procedural impropriety if there is a sufficient adverse effect on the applicant. The 'appropriate' remedy awarded by a judge for the breach of a legitimate expectation will also turn upon the adverse effects of the breach upon the applicant. The more adverse the effect, the stronger the remedy awarded.

Irrationality

Prior to Lord Diplock's third classification of 'irrationality', this ground for review used to be referred to as '*Wednesbury* unreasonableness'. Judges created a fiction by saying that, in giving a power to a decision maker, Parliament would never expect the decision maker to use the power unreasonably. Thus, if a decision maker were to use their discretionary powers unreasonably that would be acting *ultra vires* and therefore subject to judicial review.

Wednesbury unreasonableness meant that the decision maker had reached a decision no rational decision maker could have made. Thus, Lord Diplock reclassified the ground and called it 'irrationality'. Subsequent cases, however, have reflected a reluctance on the part of judges to call decisions 'irrational', given the emotive response it provokes in the decision maker. But, attempts to refer to such decisions as 'perverse' have equally met with little success.

Lord Diplock left open the possibility of the development of new grounds. In particular, he identified the concept of 'proportionality' as a possible fourth ground for judicial review. In *R v Home Office ex p Brind* (1991), judges, by majority in the House of Lords, were not prepared to extend the powers of review to challenge the proportionality of the minister's directives to the mischief at which they were aimed. It was held that proportionality was not a separate head of challenge.

Public interest immunity certificates

It is an established principle of litigation that, prior to a trial, each party has an opportunity to inspect the evidence which is to be used against them. This procedure is known as discovery. However, when one of the parties to the action happens to be the Crown, special rules apply. This enables a judge to order that documents should not be produced where disclosure would be contrary to the public interest.

Previously known as Crown privilege, public interest immunity (PII) developed predominantly through a series of civil cases. Immunity from discovery can be claimed on two grounds, the contents of the particular documents or the fact that the documents in question belong to a protected class of document.

In *Duncan v Cammel Laird* (1942), a tort action involving the death of sailors (when the submarine *Thetis* sank) in sea trials in Liverpool Bay was thwarted when the Admiralty claimed Crown privilege against disclosure of the plans used in building the submarine. In *Conway v Rimmer* (1968), judges were ready to recognise that public interest in preventing the disclosure of documents relating to national defence had also to be balanced against public interest in the administration of justice. Thus, judges decided to involve themselves in adjudicating upon whether discovery should be permitted. The mere issuing of the certificate was, therefore, no longer to be treated as being of itself conclusive. However, in *Air Canada v Secretary of State for Trade* (1983), judges in the House of Lords decided by majority that a decision by the judge to inspect the documents would be limited to instances where it is reasonably likely that the documents would assist the party seeking discovery or damage the party opposing disclosure.

Recent interest in claims of public interest immunity have heightened with the criminal trial of Paul Henderson, Trevor Abraham and Peter Allan, three directors of Matrix Churchill, a company which manufactured and exported machine tools to Iraq. In his report into the 'Arms to Iraq affair', Sir Richard Scott took the view that there was no justification for withholding evidence in criminal proceedings. Sir Nicholas Lyell, the Attorney General, had taken as his leading authority the judgment of Bingham LJ in *Makanjuola v Metropolitan Police Commissioner* (1989). In his report, however, Sir Richard Scott was of the opinion that the law was always as Lord Woolf stated it to be in the House of Lords' decision of *Wiley v Chief Constable of the West Midlands* (1994). Namely, that ministers were not obliged to sign PII certificates. They could themselves decide in favour of disclosure although if they decided against, then it would still be for the courts to ultimately decide.

Ouster clauses

```
                    |
         _____|_____
        |                       |
    PARTIAL                   TOTAL
                        (i)  'Finality'
                        (ii) 'No certiorari'
                        (iii)'Shall not be questioned'
                        (iv)'As if enacted'
```

The importance of our study of judicial review lies in the fact that it provides an effective mechanism to keep a check on the activities of our executive. Needless to say, our executive is not unaware of this fact and has produced a guide for civil servants entitled *The Judge Over Your Shoulder, Judicial Review: Balancing Scales* (1994), which warns of the dangers of judicial review.

It is not unknown for the executive to use its dominance of the legislature to try to limit or exclude the power of judicial review by inserting ouster clauses into legislation. Ouster clauses are so called for their attempt to 'oust' the jurisdiction of the judge to grant the remedy of a prerogative order against the decision maker. These clauses are 'total' or 'partial' (for example, six week time constraint) in effect. Judges tend to be hostile in their interpretation of the former and tolerant of the latter.

Differing varieties of ouster clauses which have 'total' effect have successfully been circumvented by judges. A good example of this would be the decision of judges in the

House of Lords in *Anisminic v Foreign Compensation Commission* (1969). A clause in the relevant legislation held that decisions of the Commission 'shall not be called into question in any court of law'. Using their powers of statutory interpretation, the judges interpreted this clause as only applying to a decision made within the Commission's jurisdiction. If there had been no jurisdiction to make a decision, then the clause had no effect. It was for the court to determine whether the Commission had jurisdiction or not.

Judges later went on to suggest that the effect of *Anisminic v Foreign Compensation Commission* (1969) was to hold that all errors of law inevitably went to the decision makers jurisdiction. Evidence for this can be seen in the judgment of Lord Denning MR in *Pearlman v Keepers and Governors of Harrow School* (1979). But, in *Re Recal Communications* (1981), it was held that a presumption merely existed, when a statute conferred a decision making power, that the decision maker was not intended to be the final arbiter of questions of law.

But, what of a decision maker using a power not conferred by statute?

In *R v Hull University Visitor ex p Page* (1992), it was held that whereas mandamus would lie to compel a Visitor to adjudicate on a disciplinary matter and prohibition would restrain the Visitor from acting outside their jurisdiction, certiorari would not be used for a mere error on the part of a Visitor.

In an article critical of the judgment entitled 'Visitors and error of law' (1993) LQR, Professor Sir William Wade, while acknowledging that error of law on the face of the record could 'deservedly be consigned to oblivion', and that 'the same fate has overtaken the distinction between jurisdictional and non-jurisdictional (mistakes of) law', could see little logic in applying an exception to the latter in the case of Visitors.

The justification cited by Lord Browne-Wilkinson, upholding the judgment of Lord Holt CJ in *Philips v Bury* (1694), was that an eleemosynary corporation is governed by a system of private law which is not of 'the common known laws of the kingdom' but is prescribed by the founder. This is considered by Professor Sir William Wade to be unconvincing, 'for there would seem to be no reason why the courts should not interpret university and college charters and statutes as readily as they interpret private wills, settlements and contracts'.

5 The citizen and the State

Distinguishing between rights and liberties

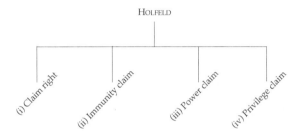

From a constitutional perspective, there is an important distinction between giving the citizens within a State legally enforceable rights, as opposed to offering legal protection of a citizen's liberties. Professor Wesley Holfeld identified four main types of claim a citizen may make:

- 'claim' right is where C claims a right and persons, generally or specifically, are under a corresponding duty to allow C access to that right;

- an 'immunity' claim is where C exercises a right and persons, generally or specifically, are under a duty not to interfere in the exercise of that right;

- a 'power' claim is where C has a right of ownership which can be exercised to create a liability. Thus, C may offer to sell the ownership rights in goods to B and thereby creates a liability;

- a 'privilege' claim merely means that C has done no wrong in exercising their liberty to do something. To Holfeld, the 'privilege' claim is the weaker claim because nobody has a duty to allow or assist C in the exercise of their liberty.

But, Holfeld's analysis is not without its critics. What Holfeld would perceive to be a weakness, Diceyan theorists see as a strength. For Professor AV Dicey, it was a fundamental feature of our constitution and its adherence to the concept of the Rule of Law that the rights of individual citizens transcend (came before) the constitution. This means that, as a citizen of the UK, you have the total freedom to do whatever it is you want to do, subject to any restriction placed upon your action in law for the benefit of the State as a whole. To Professor Dicey, this concept of residual liberties provides for better protection of an individual's freedom than any written charter. The role of the judge, therefore, is to determine on a case by case basis what restrictions the law permits for the benefit of society as a whole.

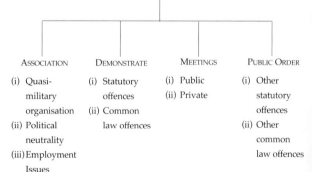

ASSOCIATION	DEMONSTRATE	MEETINGS	PUBLIC ORDER
(i) Quasi-military organisation	(i) Statutory offences	(i) Public	(i) Other statutory offences
(ii) Political neutrality	(ii) Common law offences	(ii) Private	(ii) Other common law offences
(iii) Employment Issues			

Freedom to associate, meet and demonstrate

Association

Your freedom to choose your friends, people with whom you would wish to associate, is tempered by legal restriction. There are certain categories of people that the state wishes to prevent you from associating with, for the better running of society in general.

Under the Public Order Act 1986 and the Prevention of Terrorism (Temporary Provisions) Act 1989, as amended by the Prevention of Terrorism (Additional Powers) Act 1996, special restrictions apply to associating with quasi-military organisations which have political objectives deemed detrimental to the interests of the state.

Thus, *R v Jordan and Tyndall* (1963) saw the successful prosecution of two members of the fascist group 'Spearhead', deemed a prohibited group to associate with, in accordance with s 2(1)(b) of the Public Order Act 1936. In *McEldowney v Forde* (1971), an extensive prohibition on association with republican clubs or any like organisation was upheld by judges in the House of Lords.

In accordance with the concept of the separation of powers, members of the armed forces; police; senior civil servants and judges are prohibited from active association with political groups.

Issues relating to freedom of association can also arise within the context of work. We have already seen in *Council of Civil Service Unions v Minister for the Civil Service* (1985) that staff at GCHQ, the sensitive government communications headquarters, were originally prohibited by Order in Council from any further association with their trade unions. In *Young, James and Webster v UK* (1981), the opposite problem occurred when employees were dismissed by their employer for not associating with a trade union. British Rail had entered into a 'closed-shop' agreement which was found by the European Court of Human Rights to contravene Art 11 of the European Convention on Human Rights (as it infringed freedom of choice). The resultant change in UK law renders a dismissal unlawful if one holds a deeply held conviction against association with trade unions.

Demonstrations and meetings

The significance of the freedom to associate lies in the political importance of collective strength. One means of bringing public attention to the validity of a cause is to meet and demonstrate this collective strength. Yet, this freedom often falls prey to severe restrictions deemed necessary in light of public disorder problems. For example, statutory restrictions were imposed under the Public Order Act 1936 restricting fascist marches in the east end of London in the 1930s. The Public Order Act 1986 was deemed necessary to combat the inner city riots of the 1980s and public disorder problems associated with the miners strike in 1984. Indeed, the 1986 Act, and the strengthening by the courts of police common law powers during the 1984 miners strike, means that our freedom to demonstrate is among the most severely curtailed freedoms in recent times.

The problem associated with our freedom to meet usually stems from the issue of where the meeting is supposed to take place. All land is owned by someone and, with few exceptions (see *Webster v Southwark LBC* (1983)), it is for the owners to determine whether they will permit a meeting to be held on their land. Where an owner does permit a meeting to take place on their land, *Thomas v Sawkins* (1935) proves that, irrespective of whether it is a private meeting, the police may insist on their being in attendance. Until the Public Order Act 1986, there was very little statutory control of public assemblies. Section 137 of the Highways Act 1980 places some restriction on meetings obstructing the highway, no matter how trivial the obstruction (see *Arrowsmith v Jenkins* (1963)) and *Hirst and Agu v Chief Constable of West Yorkshire* (1987). The Public Order Act 1986 and Criminal Justice and Public Order Act 1994 contain provisions which are specific to assemblies and processions, namely, ss 12–15 of the Public Order Act 1986 (as amended by the 1994 Act). Section 11 provides for the giving of notice by the organiser(s) of a public procession; s 12 allows the police to impose conditions on the said procession and, if this power is deemed insufficient, s 13 provides for the banning of all public processions or class of public procession in an area for a period of up to three months in order to maintain public order. Section 14 provides for the imposition of conditions on 'public assemblies', which is defined in s 16 as meaning 'an assembly of 20 or more persons in a public place (including the highway) which is wholly or partly open to the air'. The Criminal Justice and Public Order Act 1994 introduces the new ss 14a, 14b and 14c into the 1986 Act in order to combat 'trespassory assemblies'.

In a landmark decision on trespassory assemblies, the House of Lords held, in *DPP v Jones* (1999), that there is a public right of peaceful assembly on the highway. Interestingly, the Lord Chancellor noted in his judgment that, 'unless the common law recognises that assembly on the public highway *may* be lawful, the right contained in Art 11(1) of the [European] Convention [on Human Rights] is denied'.

Other public order offences

In addition, the Public Order Act 1986 also provides for the statutory offences of:

- riot (s 1);

- violent disorder (s 2);

- affray (s 3);

- threatening behaviour (ss 4 and 5);

- incitement to racial hatred (s 18),

which may also affect freedom of assembly. Complementing these public order offences is the offence of obstructing a police officer. In *Rice v Connolly* (1966), this offence, then contained in s 51 of the Police Act 1964, was held to be committed if one knowingly or intentionally impedes a police officer in the execution of their duty.

Police powers are further enhanced by the common law. For example, a public nuisance may arise from blocking the highway if, as in *R v Clarke (No 2)* (1964), the disruption is caused by an 'unreasonable' user of the highway. The miners' strike of 1984 saw increasing use made of the common law offence of breach of the peace. In *Moss v McLachlan* (1985), police power to regulate and control public assemblies was extended, upon the apprehension of a breach of the peace, not only to stopping vehicles and questioning the occupants but also to requiring that they discontinue their journey. Moreover, it was affirmed in *R v Home Office ex p Northumbria Police Authority* (1989) that, irrespective of the wishes of the local police authority, the Crown had a prerogative power to keep the peace which allowed the Home Secretary to 'do all that was reasonably necessary to preserve the peace of the realm'. In addition, magistrates also have a power, dating back to Justices of the Peace Act 1361, of binding over a defendant to keep the peace. The Law Commission has recommended reform of this power and there has been much recent criticism of its use against environmental protesters opposed to motorway extensions.

It should be noted that special rules govern picketing in contemplation or furtherance of a trade dispute. Section 220 of the Trade Union and Labour Relations (Consolidation) Act 1992 provides some immunity where the pickets are acting peacefully, as in *Hubbard v Pitt* (1976) at their own place of work. Such protection is lost, however, if the real intention of the pickets is to merely obstruct or harass others, as in *Thomas v NUM (South Wales)* (1986).

Freedom of expression

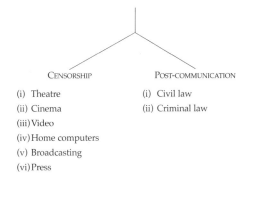

CENSORSHIP

(i) Theatre
(ii) Cinema
(iii) Video
(iv) Home computers
(v) Broadcasting
(vi) Press

POST-COMMUNICATION

(i) Civil law
(ii) Criminal law

Censorship

At one time, plays and opera were a important means of mass communication. But, as other means of mass communication developed so regulation of this area ceased to be of major importance. By the late 1950s and early 1960s, playwrights, such as John Osborne and Harold Pinter, were pushing the antiquated system of theatre censorship, via the Lord Chamberlain's office, to its limits. The Theatres Act 1968 was passed to cover live performances of a play or ballet. The Act does allow, subject to the approval of the Attorney General, for the prosecution of obscene performances. But, the reluctance to prosecute under this Act, even when prompted by campaigners, such as Mary Whitehouse (see *Romans in Britain* performed by the National Theatre in 1982), means that this is probably one of the least controlled areas of artistic expression. Any live performance not covered by the Theatres Act 1968 still comes within the ambit of the common law and thus the offences of presenting an indecent exhibition and keeping a disorderly house. In *Moores v DPP* (1991), the common law was used to restrict a live performance which involved an 'exotic dancer' having parts of his male anatomy rubbed with oil by a female member of the audience.

Early cinema film was highly combustible and therefore constituted a fire hazard to a large audience confined in a darkened space. To combat this danger the Cinematograph Act 1909 was passed which provided for the licensing of cinemas by local authorities. It was not long, however, before local authorities began using this licensing power to regulate the type of film being shown in the cinema. Thus, in 1912, the industry set up a self-censoring body, the British Board of Film Classification (BBFC), which still operates today. An 18 rating given by the Board to a film effectively means that in the opinion of the Board the film would survive a prosecution under the obscene publications legislation. But, whatever the view of the BBFC, a local authority may still refuse to grant a licence to show a film in the area under the Cinemas Act 1985 (which, together with the Local Government (Miscellaneous Provisions) Act 1982, is used to regulate sex cinemas and other sex establishments).

In the early 1980s, cinema faced competition from the rapidly growing video rental market. Despite the fact that video cassettes were covered by the obscene publications legislation, public concern over regulating the new video market resulted in the passing of the Video Recordings Act 1984 (as amended by the Criminal Justice and Public Order Act 1994), which prohibits the sale or rental of videos not classified by the BBFC. In similar fashion, public concern presently centres on the opportunities available for children to access scenes of violence or sex on their home computer.

The Broadcasting Act 1990 established a new Independent Television Commission (ITC) to replace the Independent Broadcasting Authority (IBA). This body is now charged with licensing and regulating non-BBC television. Under s 6, it must ensure that programmes are both in 'good taste and decency' and politically 'impartial'.

BBC broadcasting is not subject to this statutory restraint but is controlled by a Board of Governors, appointed by the government, which may look into such matters. However, public demonstrations of editorial interference by the Board are rare, if only because they damage the BBC's reputation for independence.

All television broadcasting now also comes under the supervision of a new Broadcasting Standards Council (BSC), which, under s 152 of the Act, draws up a code of guidance for broadcasters on how they should portray sex and violence. The government's recent decision to 'de-regulate' television with the passing of the Broadcasting Act 1990 means that we also have to take into account satellite and cable television.

At present, our press are largely subject to voluntary self-regulation (see the 'D' Notice system). The Calcutt Committee on Privacy previously recommended in 1990 that a new Press Complaints Commission (set up in 1991) replace the Press Council. Following the death of Diana, Princess of Wales, the consensus view is that editors of the press have been given one last chance to prove that voluntary self-regulation works. This was recently tested to the full with the decision of the *Sun* newspaper to publish a topless photograph of Ms Sophie Rhys-Jones, the fiancée of Prince Edward.

Civil law

One of the most important restraints on our press and broadcasting authorities is the fear of a civil action under the tort of defamation, or indeed for criminal libel. Indeed, it was a fear of this threat which prompted the passing of Art 9 of the Bill of Rights 1689, discussed in Chapter 2. Of particular importance to us, however, was the decision of judges in the House of Lords in *Derbyshire CC v Times Newspapers* (1993) when it was held, referring to leading US authorities, that local authorities and by inference government departments could not sue in libel. The *ratio decidendi* of the decision is that freedom of speech under common law is so important as to override a public body's right to maintain its reputation against improper attack.

The civil law can also be used to suppress information where that information has been acquired in 'breach of confidence'. This has a particular application to memoirs written by public servants which have national security implications, covered later in this chapter. In addition to these official secrets, there are other statutory offences against sedition; incitement to disaffection or racial hatred and blasphemy which also have an impact on free speech.

Criminal law

The most important statutory offences here are those relating to obscenity and indecency. Under s 1 of the Obscene Publications Act 1959 , an article is obscene if it has an effect:

> ... such as to tend to deprave and corrupt persons who are likely, having regard to all the circumstances, to read, see or hear the matter ...

R v Penguin Books (1961) was one of the first cases brought under the Obscene Publications Act 1959 and concerned the publication of *Lady Chatterley's Lover* by DH Lawrence. It was decided in this case that whereas the defence could not argue that there was no intention to deprave and corrupt it could, under the Act, raise the defence of 'public good', in that the article was 'in the interests of science, literature, art, learning or of other objects of general concern'. Thus, the jury should adopt a two stage approach, did the article deprave and corrupt and if so did its merits outweigh the obscenity? *DPP v Jordan* (1977) demonstrated, however, that it cannot be argued under the Act that 'hard-core' pornography has the merit of psychotherapeutic value for persons of deviant sexuality. On a further point of interpretation, it should be noted that this 'deprave and corrupt' test, as used in Obscene Publications Acts and the Theatres Act 1968, is sufficiently wide to cover not only sexual material but also drug taking (see *Calder v Powell* (1965)) and violence (see *DPP v A and BC Chewing Gum* (1968)).

Nevertheless, however wide the 'deprave and corrupt' test, it is always going to be easier to prove offences relating to 'indecency' under the Protection of Children Act 1978; Indecent Displays (Control) Act 1981 and the Customs and Excise Management Act 1979.

In addition to these statutory restraints on freedom of expression, we also need to note two common law offences, conspiracy to corrupt public morals and outraging public decency. The first of these relates to a new offence created by judges in the House of Lords in *Shaw v DPP* (1962). The creation of a new offence to corrupt public morals was the cause of much academic criticism, but, in *Knuller v DPP* (1973), judges in the House of Lords reaffirmed both the existence of this offence and another common law offence to outrage public decency. Moreover, in *R v Gibson* (1991), the offence of outraging public decency was held to apply to artistic work, notwithstanding that the offence does not permit any defence in consideration of the artistic merit of the work.

In 1979, a Home Office Committee under the chairmanship of Professor Bernard Williams published a report on obscenity and film censorship which concluded that such is the state of our law in this area 'that it is a complicated task even to piece together a statement of what the law is, let alone attempt to wrestle with or resolve the inconsistencies and anomalies'. Few would disagree that this area of our law is in need of reform, but many would disagree as to how best to reform the law.

Contempt of court

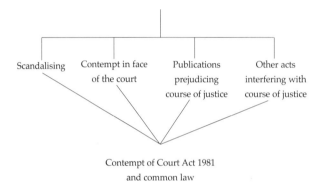

Scandalising | Contempt in face of the court | Publications prejudicing course of justice | Other acts interfering with course of justice

Contempt of Court Act 1981
and common law

However, one area of our law affecting freedom of expression which has undergone reform is contempt of court. In *AG v Times Newspapers* (1974), the parents of malformed children sued Distillers, the distributors of a morning-sickness drug called thalidomide. The *Sunday Times* campaigned on behalf of the parents arguing that the company could afford a much more generous offer of compensation than that already made. The question presented to the House of Lords was whether this amounted to contempt. The publisher and editor of the

Sunday Times took the matter to the European Commission of Human Rights and it was as a result of criticism of UK contempt laws that the Contempt of Court Act 1981 was passed. Unfortunately, this Act was not a codifying measure and thus it needs to be read in conjunction with rules of contempt under the common law. The main categories under which one may be held to be in contempt of court today are scandalising the court; contempt in the face of the court or publishing material which prejudices the course of justice.

Freedom from interference to your person or property

| Stop and search | Arrest | Search and seizure of property | Detention |

In determining the degree of balance between personal liberty and the criminal justice system, three issues need to be considered. We should seek to ensure that the innocent defendant is not convicted. One way of achieving this is simply by not convicting any defendant. This would of course also be unacceptable because another interest of the criminal justice system is to ensure the conviction of the guilty. Both these factors have also to be considered in the light of economic use of resources.

The 1970s had seen a spate of miscarriages of justice, citizens whose personal liberty have been wrongfully denied by the State. In response to growing public concern, a Royal Commission was set up and reported in 1981 on inadequacies in criminal procedures for the safeguarding of suspects. At the time, there were no clear powers for the police to stop, search and arrest suspects or enter into premises. Thus, the Police and Criminal Evidence Act (PACE) 1984 was introduced with the purpose of putting police powers on a clear statutory footing and at the same time providing greater procedural safeguards for suspects.

Rules are made under the Act which constrain the police in the operation of their formidable powers. In addition to these rules, there are Codes of Practice made under the Act (later revised)

- Code A: stop and search procedures;

- Code B: searching of premises;

- Code C: detention and interviewing;

- Code D: identification;

- Code E: tape recording.

Contained within the Codes of Practice are separate Notes for Guidance. There are numerous Home Office Circulars, some for use with PACE, others which are free standing which need also to be taken into account.

It should be noted here that whereas the aforementioned has a general application there is a special class of suspect for which differing rules may apply. Due to the seriousness of the threat to the State, the Prevention of Terrorism (Temporary Provisions) Act 1989 (as amended by the Prevention of Terrorism (Additional Powers) Act 1996) often makes special provisions for the terrorist suspect.

Further public disquiet with the criminal justice system in the wake of more recent miscarriages of justice (Guildford Four, Birmingham Six, etc) led to the setting up of a Royal

Commission on Criminal Justice in 1993 under the chairmanship of Lord Runciman. However, a number of findings of the Commission were not adhered to by the government.

In particular, ss 34–37 of the Criminal Justice and Public Order Act 1994 now curtails the suspect's right to silence, in that inference may now be drawn from the suspect's silence in court.

The interpretation a judge is to put to a jury on this curtailed right to silence was explored recently in the cases of *R v N* (1998) and *R v Daniel* (1998). Whereas the decision in *R v N* (1998) limits the circumstances in which an adverse reference can be drawn from the silence of the suspect, *R v Daniel* confirms the danger to a suspect of relying upon legal advice to stay silent. It will be interesting to see whether this precedent survives the Human Rights Act 1998 and the introduction into our domestic law of Art 6.

Stop and search

A legal power to stop a suspect is contained in a number of statutes, such as the Misuse of Drugs Act 1971; Sporting Events (Control of Alcohol) Act 1985; Road Traffic Act 1988 and the Criminal Justice and Public Order Act 1994, etc. However, if we confine ourselves to PACE, then, under s 1, a police officer has such a power if there is 'reasonable suspicion' (to be assessed to an objective standard by the judge; see *Lyons v Chief Constable of West Yorkshire* (1997)) that stolen goods, offensive weapons or other prohibited articles may be found. Your safeguards as a suspect lie in the fact that this power will have been used unlawfully if the officer failed to follow the procedural requirements of ss 2 and 3 and Code A. Thus, before the stop and search the officer should give you:

... his name and the name of the police station to which he is attached; the object of the proposed search; the constable's grounds for proposing to make it.

In addition, the officer should make a record of the search on the spot, or as soon as is practicable, to which you should have access.

Arrest

The State gives a police officer a power to arrest you either with or without an arrest warrant. A warrant for your arrest may be issued by a magistrate under s 1 of the Magistrates' Courts Act 1980. The police officer may also arrest you under s 24 and s 25 of PACE without the need for a warrant. Section 24 is used for serious offences and may be used where the officer has reasonable grounds to suspect that one of the offences covered by the section is being, is about to be or has been committed. Recent additions to the list of offences have been made by the Offensive Weapons Act 1996 and the Crime and Disorder Act 1998. In similar fashion, s 25 covers other offences if specific conditions, 'the general arrest conditions', exist. Your safeguards as a suspect lie in the fact that a power to arrest must exist and the procedural requirements of s 28 of PACE should be adhered to. Thus, you should be informed of your arrest and the reasons for it at the time, or as soon as is practicable (see *Dawes v DPP* (1994)). This will also apply to other statutory powers of arrest without warrant, such as ss 12 and 14 of the Public Order Act 1986.

At common law, the power to arrest for breach of the peace is unaffected by PACE. *Foulkes v Chief Constable of Merseyside* (1998) has clarified the common law powers of arrest where no actual breach of the peace has transpired. In such circumstances, a power of arrest is held only to exist if 'a sufficiently real and present threat' of a breach of the peace is apprehended.

Under s 117 of PACE, the officer may only use reasonable force to arrest you in order to effect a valid arrest.

Search and seizure of property

Under s 17 of PACE, a power exists to enter a home to effect an arrest, although *O'Loughlin v Chief Constable of Essex* (1997) would imply that caution must be exercised when gaining entry by force. Under s 18 of PACE, immediately after an arrest, an officer can, if there are reasonable grounds for suspecting that evidence exists in connection with the arrest which is not protected by legal privilege, search a premises (see *Krohn v DPP* (1997)). A power exists under the foregoing section and s 19 of PACE for the officer to seize your goods if there are reasonable grounds for believing they have been obtained in consequence of an offence or that they are evidence of an offence which it is necessary to seize in order to prevent their concealment, adjustment, loss or destruction. Under Code B, if the search is made with your consent, you should signify that fact by signing a Notice of Powers and Rights. If not with your consent, you should be informed of the purpose and grounds of the search. With regard to demanding a right of entry into your home for the purposes of searching it not associated with arrest, the police officer may obtain a search warrant from a magistrate under s 8 of PACE. We have already noted from *Rice v Connolly* (1966) that any attempt to obstruct the above searches will be an offence.

We might also note that other statutes, such as the Chemical Weapons Act 1996, can also be used to authorise entry into a premises. *McLeod v Metropolitan Police Commissioner* (1994) demonstrates the power of a police officer, under the common law, to enter private property in order to prevent a breach of the peace.

Detention
Upon an arrest, a person will be taken to be detained at a police station. Section 37(2) of PACE makes clear that the purpose of such a detention is to secure a confession. This detention period can be up to 24 hours, increasing to 96 hours for a serious arrestable offence (or up to seven days under the Prevention of Terrorism (Temporary Provisions) Act 1989, as amended by the Prevention of Terrorism (Additional Powers) Act 1996). Once in detention at the police station, any police interviewing should be conducted in accordance Codes C and E. The significant safeguards here are that a suspect should be cautioned; a contemporaneous recording/tape recording made of the interview with an opportunity for you to read over and sign the record of the interview; the notification and the right to legal advice and, where appropriate, the presence of an adult. However, in *DPP v L* (1999), it was held that the custody officer was under no duty to investigate the legality of the arrest and could assume it was lawful.

Police impropriety

Exclusion of evidence   Damages   Police complaints

CONSTITUTIONAL LAW

It is apparent from the aforementioned that the police enjoy considerable powers to restrict a person's liberty. Such extensive powers are necessary to facilitate the effective policing of our State. Thus, our constitutional safeguards as potential suspects lie not in the restriction of the scope of the power but more in the supervision of the 'reasonable' exercise of these powers. But, what penalty awaits the law enforcement officer who acts unreasonably in the exercise of their powers?

Exclusion of evidence

In addition to any writ of habeas corpus or claims to self-defence which may be applicable, the first redress one may have for police impropriety could be the refusal of the judge to allow evidence to be used. If a confession has been extracted, a police officer using oppressive tactics, it can be excluded by the judge under s 76(2)(a) of PACE. Indeed, the case of the 'Cardiff Three' demonstrates the power of judges in the Court of Appeal to quash convictions due to oppressive questioning. If in other ways a confession has been extracted in circumstances conducive of unreliability, the judge may exclude it under s 76(2)(a) of PACE. The judge also has a power to exclude a confession if admitting it might create unfairness at the trial. Section 78 of PACE allows for the exclusion of physical evidence if the police officer obtained the evidence with deliberate illegality. We should note that s 82 of PACE still retains a discretion for the judge under the common law to exclude evidence.

Damages

A second redress may be to institute a claim for damages against the police. Breach of the statutory arrest or detention rules may give grounds to a claim for damages for false imprisonment. The excessive use of force by a police officer may lead to a claim for damages for assault and battery and a right to prosecute the police officer. Trespass to land or to goods may occur if the police officer fails to follow the statutory rules relating to search and seizure. Finally, a tort action for malicious prosecution will be available if the police have abused their powers in recommending a prosecution.

Formal compliant

The third method by which one may seek a redress for police impropriety is to institute a formal complaint against the police officer with the police themselves. Here, the police officer may be internally disciplined for breaches of the codes. However, it is generally agreed that this complaints procedure (with the supervision of the Police Complaints Authority in allegations of serious misconduct) lacks the trust of both the general public and the police themselves as an effective means of the redress a grievance.

National security

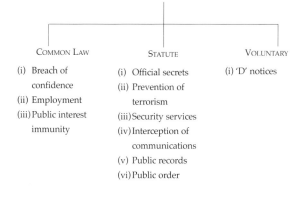

COMMON LAW	STATUTE	VOLUNTARY
(i) Breach of confidence	(i) Official secrets	(i) 'D' notices
(ii) Employment	(ii) Prevention of terrorism	
(iii) Public interest immunity	(iii) Security services	
	(iv) Interception of communications	
	(v) Public records	
	(vi) Public order	

We have already seen that issues of national security permeate a wide range of areas. In the employment field, we saw in *Council of Civil Service Unions v Minister for the Civil Service* (1985) the use of national security to defeat a legal challenge to the banning of trade unions at GCHQ. In the study of our freedom of association and assembly, we noted the effect of public order legislation and other common law offences. The case of *Malone v Metropolitan Police Commissioner* (1979) raised the issue of State interception of communications and prompted the passing of the Interception of Communications Act 1985.

Deportation orders have also been served in the interest of national security. In *R v Home Secretary ex p Hosenball* (1977), a deportation order was made against an American journalist who proposed publishing an article about how our government monitored communications. *R v Home Secretary ex p Cheblak* (1991) saw a deportation order made, during the Gulf hostilities, against a person who had lived in this country since 1975. In both instances, the government refused to furnish further information to the court, justifying their decisions again on the grounds of national security.

The Prevention of Terrorism Bill was passed in 24 hours and within eight days of the Birmingham pub bombings in November 1974, without virtual amendment or dissent. This legislation was the forerunner to the Prevention of Terrorism (Temporary Provisions) Act 1989, as amended by the Prevention of Terrorism (Additional Powers) Act 1996 (which itself completed its passage through both Houses of Parliament in two days). Notices censoring the broadcasting of certain political views from Northern Ireland have been made, in the interests of national security, under the Broadcasting Act 1981 (see *R v Home Secretary ex p Brind* 1991)). National security considerations were also inherent in the issuing of the Matrix Churchill PII certificates.

Yet, nowhere is the UK attitude to national security better illustrated than in the individual's right of access to sensitive State information. The Official Secrets Act 1991 was hurriedly passed by Parliament in response to a general fear about spying. The case of *Chandler v DPP* (1964) demonstrated, however, the wide terms used in the Act when it was held to cover a CND demonstration at a US military air base in this country. After continued public disquiet, the Franks Committee in 1972 recommended repeal of the Act because of its unacceptably wide drafting and 'catch-all' provisions. It was not until *R v Ponting* (1985) and his acquittal by the jury for leaking information to Parliament about the sinking of the Argentine battleship *General Belgrano*, however, that the government accepted the need to reform the Act.

The new Official Secrets Act 1989 divides the protected information into specific categories:

- security and intelligence (s 1);

- defence (s 2);

- international relations (s 3);

- criminal investigations (s 4).

The Act requires that the leak of information needs to be a 'damaging' disclosure in order to initiate a prosecution. Certain defences are also permitted, but not the defence of 'public interest', as raised by Clive Ponting.

In addition to these restrictions placed on the access to information under the criminal law, the civil law also allows for restriction under breach of confidence. Instances of its operation would include *AG v Jonathan Cape* (1976) and the numerous instances of litigation associated with the book, *Spycatcher*. The UK Press were less than happy with the outcome of the *Spycatcher* litigation and took the matter to the European Commission of Human Rights. In *Observer v UK* (1991), the Court held that the failure of the House of Lords to discharge the injunctions in *AG v Guardian Newspapers* (1987), when the book was already available in the USA, violated Art 10 of the European Convention on Human Rights.

Yet, recent attempts have been made by successive governments to promote greater openness. Following on from the publication of a White Paper on *Open Government* in 1993, the then Premier, John Major, offered an insight into the structure of Cabinet government and its Committees. The security services have, for the first time, been placed on an open statutory footing with the Security Services Act 1989 and the Intelligence Services Act 1994. The present government has also introduced, in May 1999, a draft Freedom of Information Bill. This is intended to supersede the Code of Practice on Access to Government Information and amend the Data Protection Act 1998.

Whereas the aforementioned may represent small steps, at least they are seen by many to at least be steps in the right direction.

Human Rights Act 1998

Passed by the House of Commons on 21 October 1998 and receiving Royal Assent on 9 November 1998, the Human

Rights Act 1998 has been heralded by David Pannick QC as being 'the jewel in the crown of this government's programme of constitutional reform'.

According to Lord Irvine, the Lord Chancellor, the origins of this Act are to be found in the government's perception that:

> ... the traditional freedom of the individual under an unwritten constitution, to do himself that which is not prohibited by law, gives inadequate protection from misuse of power by the State ... that is why we were determined to introduced a rights based system under which peoples' rights were asserted as positive entitlements expressed in clear and principled terms.

Section 3 of the Human Rights Act 1998 introduces a new rule of construction requiring that, 'as far as it is possible to do so', both primary and subordinate legislation must be read and given effect by British judges in a way which is compatible with Arts 2–12 and 14 of the European Convention on Human Rights (hereafter referred to as Convention rights).

In instances where subordinate legislation is found to be incompatible with Convention rights, British judges will have the additional power to set the inconsistent provisions aside to the extent which is necessary to allow full effect to be given to Convention rights.

Nevertheless, in recognition of parliamentary sovereignty, s 3 provides that the interpretative obligation of this Act does not affect the validity, continuing operation of enforcement of any incompatible primary legislation. Thus, the Human Rights Act 1998 cannot be used to strike down any part of an existing statute or being 'unconstitutional'. If primary legislation is held to be incompatible with Convention rights, British judges will still have to enforce it.

Nevertheless, s 4 of the Human Rights Act 1998 does provide for certain higher courts to make a declaration that it is not possible to construe the primary legislation to harmonise with Convention rights. If the courts do invoke their powers under s 4 to make such a declaration, s 10 of the Human Rights Act 1998 comes into play. This provides for a minister to make amendments to the offending legislation by means of a 'fast track' parliamentary procedure. But, this opportunity for a minister to initiate amendments to primary legislation, outside of the normal parliamentary process, is only limited to instances where there are 'compelling reasons' to do so.

Additionally, in accordance with s 19 of the Act, every minister charged with the conduct of a Bill through Parliament is now required to make and publish a written statement before the second reading in each House about the compatibility of the proposed legislation with Convention rights.

Section 7 of the Human Rights Act 1998 allows a person who is, or will be, the 'victim' of a breach of Convention rights by a 'public authority' to bring proceedings against that authority. Under s 6, Convention rights are only binding against 'public authorities', which are widely defined as bodies having a 'partly public function'. In accordance with s 8, such a victim may seek:

> ... such relief or remedy or ... order ... as [the Court] considers just and appropriate.

An account of the intended operation of the Human Rights Act 1998 is given by Helen Fenwick in the *Student Law Review* (Spring 1999 issue, Vol 26). In the first instance, it is anticipated that there will be sufficient flexibility within the rules of construction to avoid the requirement of a declaration of incompatibility. Thus, s 10 of the Contempt of Court Act 1981 was found by the European Court of Human Rights in *Goodwin v UK* (1996) to be incompatible with Art 10 of the European Convention. Yet, all that a British judge is required to do is use s 3 of the Human Rights Act 1998 to re-interpret s 10 of the Contempt of Court Act 1981 in light of the *Goodwin* ruling and thus avoid any need for a declaration of incompatibility.

But, in situations where incompatibility cannot be avoided, limitations within the Human Rights Act 1998 start to become apparent.

Convention rights can only be enforced under s 6 against 'public authorities'. Thus, private bodies (for example, national newspapers) remain unaffected by the Act. Further, s 7 of the Act clearly precludes pressure groups from becoming 'victims' of the breach of a Convention right under the Act.

Only certain higher courts have the power to make a declaration of incompatibility under s 4; yet, where is the incentive for the 'victim' to take the matter to the higher courts when that court remains obliged to enforce incompatible domestic legislation?

Even if a declaration of incompatibility is made by a higher court, a minister is not obliged to make any amendments. The fact that a declaration has been made is not in itself a 'compelling reason' for doing so.

Under s 2 of the Human Rights Act 1998, British judges 'must take into account' any relevant Strasbourg jurisprudence such as the complex concepts of proportionality and the margin of appreciation, but they are not bound by it. Moreover, if, in accordance with s 19, a minister makes clear that provisions within a Bill are intended to conflict with Convention rights, a British judge must be presumed to allow the legislation to purposefully override the Convention rights.

Despite these obvious limitations, commentators welcome the Human Rights Act 1998 and look forward, in the words of Lord Woolf, Master of the Rolls:

> ... to this legislation energising the whole of the United Kingdom's legal system with effects felt across the breadth of both civil and criminal justice.

Indeed, for many the principal concern has now become the delay in bringing the Act into effect.

David Pannick QC noted that:

> ... predictions of the date for implementation have become progressively pessimistic. The earliest date now being considered by ministers is summer 2000, and there are rumours that the Home Office and other departments are keen to delay until mid-2001.

But, what is the cause of such delay in bringing into effect an Act which is already on the statute book?

The problem would appear to be one of impact and adjustment. Whilst observing that rights have to be offset by responsibilities and obligations, Professor John Griffiths, writing in the *Guardian* newspaper in April 1999, noted:

> ... the heart of the problem of this highly problematic Act of Parliament ... [is] ... it is a political statute requiring answers to political questions. No rights are absolute. All rights are relative and relating ... nothing is sacred. Everything is political.

Perhaps the last word should be left to Lord Irvine, the Lord Chancellor, who, in delivering the 1999 Paul Sieghart Memorial Lecture entitled 'Activism and Restraint: Human Rights and the Interpretative Process' confidently asserted:

> ... the typology of change in English public law is one of evolution, not revolution ... the existing corpus of administrative law ... form(s) a firm foundation on which to build the super-structure of a new, rights based public law for Britain in the 21st century ... A former Chief Justice of the US Supreme Court famously remarked that a 'constitution is that the judges say it is'. More recently, Sir Stephen Sedley observed that 'the reverse is true as well: if the judges are not prepared to speak for it, a constitution is nothing'.